AGE SPEAKS
FOR ITSELF

AGE SPEAKS FOR ITSELF

Silent Voices of the Elderly

Tom Koch

Westport, Connecticut
London

Library of Congress Cataloging-in-Publication Data

Koch, Tom, 1949–
    Age speaks for itself : silent voices of the elderly / Tom Koch.
      p.   cm.
    Includes bibliographical references.
    ISBN 0–275–96796–4 (alk. paper)
    1. Aged—United States.   2. Aging—United States.   3. Old age—
United States.   I. Title.
HQ1064.U5K63   2000
305.26′0973—dc21   99–37529

British Library Cataloguing in Publication Data is available.

Library of Congress Catalog Card Number: 99–37529
ISBN: 0–275–96796–4

First published in 2000

Praeger Publishers, 88 Post Road West, Westport, CT 06881
An imprint of Greenwood Publishing Group, Inc.
www.praeger.com

Printed in the United States of America

The paper used in this book complies with the
Permanent Paper Standard issued by the National
Information Standards Organization (Z39.48–1984).

10 9 8 7 6 5 4 3 2 1

Copyright Acknowledgments

The author and publisher gratefully acknowledge permission for use of the following material:

"An Irish Airman Foresees His Death" from *The Collected Works of W. B. Yeats, Vol. I: The Poems*. Revised and edited by Richard J. Finneran (New York: Scribner), and *Selected Poems and Two Plays of William Butler Yeats*. Edited and Introduction by M. L. Rosenthal (New York: Collier, 1962). Reprinted with permission of Simon & Schuster and AP Watt Ltd.

"Under Ben Bulben" fron *Selected Poems and Two Plays of William Butler Yeats*. Edited and Introduction by M. L. Rosenthal (New York: Collier, 1962). Reprinted with permission of AP Watt Ltd.

An earlier version of chapter 5 was originally published in Tom Koch, *A Place in Time: Care Givers for Their Elderly* (Westport, CT: Praeger, 1993).

Contents

Acknowledgments

Books result not from the solitary efforts of writers but from the communal labors of a wide range of people. This is especially true in a series whose basis is the lived life of narrators involved in challenging, vexing, frustrating events. Like its predecessor, *A Place in Time,* this book was made possible by the narrators who gave freely of their time and welcomed me into their homes and their histories. Their openness and generosity has taught me much; their histories have educated me in the process. My gratitude to them and others whose lives have informed this series is great.

Authors write manuscripts, which are transformed into books through the labor of people who work for publishers. The transformation of my writings into this trilogy was made possible through the labors of a large cast of professionals at Praeger Books. Vice-president James T. Sabin has been my editor from the start. He believed in these works even when I was uncertain, encouraged me when possible and fought for the works among his colleagues where it was necessary. Production supervisor Catherine Lyons worked hard to make sure the first books in this trilogy were both accurate and attractive, a job passed in this volume to Heidi Straight. It was their sometimes herculean task to assure the work's transformation from a writer's project into a project that would be widely disseminated to the public-at-large. I thank them both for their efforts. Elsewhere in the Greenwood/Praeger pantheon are a legion of people who, like Norma Johnson, have assisted me in securing the rights to quotes and excerpts, and marketing specialists who have worked to assure the book's widest dissemination. Theirs is the final, necessary effort that propels a work forward.

Over the years I have heard from readers around the world who were touched by *Mirrored Lives'* story of parental care, involved with *A Place in Time's* presentation of the issues surrounding elder care, or involved through this or that article of mine on these subjects. Each reader's comments—praise or criticism has helped me better understand the complex of events that is age and aging in our world. To all those who have written and commented . . . thank you.

Finally, a special thanks is due to Dr. Bill McArthur of Vancouver. It was through him that I met two of the narrators included in this volume, through his expertise that I came to understand the problems that occur at the meeting place of age and illness. For more than a decade he has served as an informed technical advisor, advocate, and counselor. Nobody could ask for a more generous or exacting tutor. This book is affectionately dedicated to him, and to the seniors whose lives have informed us both.

Introduction:
"Nothing Fails Like
Success"

Who would have believed that a time might come when a man like me would regard the day of his death as better than the day of his birth? Nothing fails like success.[1]

Joseph Heller, *God Knows*[1]

We do not like our seniors, nor do we understand them. They are wrinkled, shrunken in stature, and speak too often in dry, querulous voices. Our assumptions of physical beauty and social responsibility are violated by the elderly, who rarely work and are free of the obligations that plague us younger adults. "It is old age, rather than death that is to be contrasted with life," wrote Simone de Beauvoir.[2] "Old age is life's parody." And so we (and often they themselves) see it, today. Like ungainly, assertive adolescents, retirees are frustrating and vexing challenges to the model of adulthood that society holds dear. We tolerate teenagers who, if they survive, will become adults like us—people with families and responsibilities and jobs. But the elderly have no such potential, and so we ask ourselves whether they should exist at all.

We cherish our children and appreciate our contemporaries in ways that exclude our oldest relations. They are present and future. Seniors are only the past. The individual retiree may be accepted within our lives, however, even if the elderly are, as a class, disavowed. Old Aunt Margaret is appreciated for the cookies she still bakes every Christmas for us all, for that minimal service that she still provides.³ And we maintain a reflexive, distanced affection for Uncle Ralph, the boring fellow with interminable stories of a time we never knew. He is an inconsequential but somehow comforting constant in our world. That Grandma Clarisse still gets around, alone, at the age of eighty-nine is an inspiration, of course. Why, I saw her last Thanksgiving at Aunt Mildred's home. I'm sure I'd have heard if she were ill.

We may love an individual senior, yet dislike seniority as a general condition because it reminds us that, in Joseph Heller's words, "Nothing fails like success." The frail old man shambling forward in his walker; the osteoporotic woman bent to the shape of a question mark by the weight of gravity on frail bones; the androgynous crone who sits quietly in the park all Wednesday, the one for whom feeding pigeons is a favored activity: all are the winners of life's race for survival. As such, they are a warning, a promise that what we most want we will never have. The eternal present of the healthy, contented, able adult is a dream that will necessarily end. Work ends, health fails, and, sooner or later, even love dies. The best result that any can hope for is that the subjects of our contemporary commitments—people or jobs or activities—will end before us and that we will be left as no more than guardians of a progressively solitary past. The most fortunate among us can expect only a healthy maturity of work and friends, a life of responsibility and family that will last no more than a few decades. It is that truth—demanding and immutable—that so many people see in the individual, fragile senior. It is the harsh fact of mortality that we fear. Seniors remind us by their stories and, perversely, by their fragile survival that we, too, will end. Our time will pass and our triumphs be thus diminished just as their age has ended. Is it any wonder we feel in equal measure dislike, disdain, and disaffection?

What we who are younger know is that we do not want to die, but neither do we want to be like the old, forgetful woman who lives next door or the man in the wheelchair who lives down the street with Parkinson's disease as his principle companion. His wife died a decade ago, after their two sons moved away to other cities, other lives. He's the one with the visiting nurse whose car is parked, three days out of five, before the house that was once filled with children but now stands silent and a bit neglected. We fear the immobile oldster sitting for interminable hours on the porch of the nursing home, bored attendant by his side; the person we see, some days, as we walk home from work. If that is the future, we think, longevity isn't worth the effort (constant exercise, careful diet, plus refusal of nicotine and excessive alcohol use) it requires in the present. In the end, we are more afraid of advanced age than we are of the death that must be, sooner or later, its inevitable companion.

Our fear and dislike take many forms, some more overt than others. There is elder abuse, a subject much in the news: physical assault, financial exploitation, and emotional battery are its most common forms. As devastating for many seniors is the more general abuse of elder neglect, a systematic absence of regard that says to the senior, "Hey, you're not my responsibility. I have important things to do. You're an adult. Fend for yourself." Unlike elder abuse, neglect is not legally actionable. It sometimes manifests as the "packed-suitcase syndrome," when younger relatives dump grandmother or grandfather at the emergency room door—suitcases ready—with the simple statement that "I can't care for him (or her) anymore."[4]

More generally, it is the constant of "I'm busy," when invited to visit and perhaps dine at the old, ancestral home; when company is requested and offered together. Socially, elder neglect means that still able seniors cannot expect work commensurate with their background or experience. As retirees, the best they can hope for after mandatory retirement is a counter job at a McDonald's restaurant. Like nineteenth-century factory workers who began and ended their jobs as lowly sweepers on some shop floor, our seniors' last post is the same as their first: minimum wage at the soda fountain pushing colas, milkshakes, and burgers.

Finally, systematic neglect occurs when we do not listen, when we reduce seniors to a Cheshire cat-like appendage to our worlds. We may perceive their bodies, but we do not hear their words because their perspective is discounted from the start. Simply, we do not listen. The elderly are silent speakers whose complex perspective is lost to us in the advancing, busy present. They are echoes of past events we refuse to perceive, palimpsests of past lives whose relevance to contemporary affairs is reflexively ignored. If their arguments are acknowledged at all, it is rarely with more than a condescending, dismissive air. Ours is a culture focused not on being but on becoming—on the future rather than the past that grounds and will define it. And because we seek that future, we fear those whose lives speak too forcefully of what has been. Who cares what they say or feel? It's not yesterday we seek, but tomorrow.

This is a new attitude. Less than a century ago, age and its perspective were a sought-after, honored state. We respected those few who were fortunate enough to experience it. But in the postindustrial world we have redefined aging as a process of obsolescence, of necessary weakness and continued decline. As Tamara Haraven pointed out in an article more timely today than it was on its publication in 1976, what was once the triumph of the "survival of the fittest" (or at least the most fortunate) has become an unseemly condition of dependence and deterioration.[5] This is not a matter of simple biology or of social necessity but the result of cultural choice and social definition.

THE ELDER CLASS

Ironically, the creation of a class of seniors who have survived sixty-five or seventy years is also one of this century's greater achievements. Miraculous advances in medical science and technology have extended the average life span in Western society in an unprecedented way. "Old age is the most unexpected of all things that happen to a man," Leon Trotsky said in 1935.[6] But what was rare and unusual only two generations ago has become commonplace on the cusp of the millennium. To die at sixty or sixty-five years, today, is to die "before one's time." Medicine has vanquished diseases and controlled debilitating conditions that, in 1920, limited the average North American's life expectancy to fifty-four years. By the mid-1990s, that life span had been extended to seventy-five years of age.[7] At the same time, postmodern society created sufficient wealth for a generation of aging retirees to spend their last decades in a leisure our retirement laws have imposed on them all.

The result has been a fundamental change in society, the expansion of a once minuscule "elite of elders,"[8] seniors who were seen as special solely because they had survived into an expanding class of aging citizens with which society is uneasy. We honored the former because they were exceptional, indulged them because they were rarities. As such, they represented no real threat to our vision of how the world should be. Today, however, the elderly man or woman is just another "greedy geezer," spending our inheritance, the burden of a "sandwich generation" with better things to do than care for some old fart.[9] Like many seniors themselves, we are caught between the potential richness of lives that will extend into their seventies and their eighties, and a fear of the fragilities and losses that most believe continuity necessarily carries with it.

One response has been to define seniors as those who have used up their fair measure of our communal resources. They're the ones who had their chance and now are, at best, superfluous. Some academics call this the "fair innings" argument, one that suggests that we all have our chance at bat, and, by definition, all seniors have had their chance. That is the view of politicians like Richard Lamm[10] and ethicists like Daniel Callahan[11] who, in the 1980s, suggested that health care be rationed in such a way as to exclude seniors from expensive treatments that would prolong their life. And at the level of the family, there are the brothers and sisters who shrug and ask, when Dad requires rehabilitation following a stroke or Mom needs surgery for breast cancer, "What for? What's the point?"

We assume that age equals weakness, that seniority means uselessness, and that to grow old is to grow away from the activities that have sustained us across the decades. What we do not ask is how we shall define the moment when growing and maturing become failing and declining. If gericide—or at least benign neglect—is to become an official policy, at what age will it commence? When is old too old, and why must active and social contribution end because a person lives past the age of fifty, sixty, or seventy years? These are the questions each generation must ask. At what date in our lives, and the lives of our neighbors, does the success of survival become the burden of continuance? If survival is indeed a burden, after which birthday do the benefits of accumulated experience become merely the boring remembrances of the irrelevant old?

We have created a class of elderly whose characteristics are fragility, dependence, societal expense, and social redundancy. That the characteristics of this greater class may bear no relation to an individual member is a fact generally ignored by the social scientists who study them, the ethicists who debate their social value, and, often, by seniors themselves. One purpose of this project is to insist on the individual reality within the broad context of social definition, to question the general perspective through a detailed description of the individual case.

Because the idea of a society of seniors is a new phenomenon—we have yet to decide where seniors can or should fit into our greater world. "Grow old along with me," Robert Browning urged, "the best is yet to be/the last for which the first was made." Is there something distinct about a later stage of life to which those early decades necessarily point? Perhaps the last years need be little different from the preceding decades. Is seniority a unique and wonderful achievement or is it an unseemly, biological mistake in which an oldster becomes, somehow, a parody of his or her earlier, younger self?

Television commercials, arbiters of our age, answer the question definitively. From June Allyson's cheerful shilling for adult diapers in the 1980s to Martha Raye's enthusiastic endorsement in the 1990s for denture adhesives, we know what to think. Old folks are a Raggedy Ann-style people who are less than the sum of their failing, individual parts. Toothless and incontinent, they are a core of rheumatism surrounded by a field of loneliness to be assuaged by a kindly telephone company permitting a grand-child's distanced voice to brighten some old person's otherwise featureless day. And if there is no call, no matter. Oldsters have no more urgent business than to sit and wait for the phone to ring. In the interim, they can contemplate dentures that do not fit, bladders whose muscles are no longer adequate, and the promises for "peace of mind" regularly bulk mailed to seniors by life insurance companies and funeral homes.

AGE AS PATHOLOGY

We have defined age as a disability and longevity as a pathological condition. With de Beauvoir, we assume, reflexively, that, "In a life whose fire has died, they have been." But no law of nature insists that interest and passion must end after a person's forty-fifth, sixty-fifth, or eighty-fifth birthday. It is teenagers, not seniors, who most typically commit suicide because they see no future to their lives. Ennui and hubris are malaises more common to middle-aged adults than to seniors. To define the elderly by their increasing proximity to death, or by a specific disability, is to ignore the fact that one may die at any age, and at every age life may be seriously restricted by an incapacitating illness or a loss of hope.

A man in his thirties with Amyotrophic Lateral Sclerosis (ALS), the progressive, paralyzing condition also known as Lou Gehrig's disease, needs the same high levels of care we reflexively assume only fragile seniors will require. A woman in her forties with multiple sclerosis may be no less needy than the seventy-five-year-old person confined to a wheelchair by arthritis and osteoporosis. If "cost of care" were the criterion, people with AIDS would be subjects of medical discrimination, not support and concern. Indeed, the sole virtue that attends to the equation of age and illness is that it buffers us from the knowledge that a host of disabling conditions—some fatal, some not—place our own, younger lives at risk. "I'm safe," we say. "I'm not old. *They're* the ones unable to fend for themselves."

Age and its relations are largely a matter of social definition. "Age and aging are related to biological phenomena," as Tamara Haraven observed twenty years ago, "but the meanings of age and aging are socially and culturally determined."[12] Seniority results in a series of physical changes that range from changing skin texture and decreasing bone density to diminished audible acuity and the almost inevitable need for reading glasses. Continuance means a statistically increased risk of specific illnesses.[13] Some of these can be delayed or minimized by life style, medicine, and cosmetics, but, sooner or later, most are the inevitable companion of survival.

Similarly, there are diseases largely restricted to the survivors among us, from chronic lymphocytic leukemia—once called "senile leukemia"—to Alzheimer's disease. So what? In any other context, definition (and discrimination) on the basis of susceptibility to a particular disease would be decried reflexively as unacceptable prejudice. We do not despise African Americans because they are susceptible to sickle-cell anemia. Nor do we condemn persons of Eastern European, Jewish descent for a genetic vulnerability to Tay-Sachs syndrome. Only the elderly are defined by us on the basis of medical vulnerability and thus the potential burden of their assumed fragility.

"We are told over and over," writes gerontologist David P. Barash, "that age equals weakness."[14] There is nothing new in this. "What a train of woes—and such woes—comes with a prolonged old age," lamented Juvenal in his *Tenth Satire*. "To begin with, this deformed, hideous, unrecognizable face; this vile leather instead of skin; these pendulous cheeks; these wrinkles like those around the mouth of an old she-ape as she sits scratching in the shady Thabaracan woods." That Juvenal's oldster was almost surely under fifty years of age is a fact too easily forgotten in our time. After all, in his day, the life span of an average citizen was under thirty years. Only scholars remember where that forest was, but all today are familiar with the unflattering portrait of society's most senior citizens. If we must "recognize ourselves in this old man or in that old woman," as Simone de Beauvoir insisted, it is not a meeting we ever have relished.

Although fragile seniors have been portrayed in an unflattering light for millennia, it is our utilitarian generation that has chosen to define them almost exclusively as a burden to society and their families. The elderly are no longer perceived as vessels of wisdom and conveyors of our shared history, but as expensive offshoots of a science that is out of control. To fight for life past a "normal life span," the argument goes, is to create an expensive class of unproductive seniors who absorb resources that should go to younger folks.

"Do not let young children suffer," David Lamm pleaded in the 1980s, "because of health care we give the elderly." His *Ten Commandments of an Aging Society* was a popular call to concentrate social resources on younger citizens and at the expense of seniors.[15] Lamm's assumption—utilitarian and exact—was that youth is more valuable than seniority. Seniors are expensive. Therefore, one must be sacrificed for the other. This is *homo economicus*, humans as economic ciphers whose value can be defined in economic terms. Is this all we are, however? If so, many who are younger, poorer, and more needy would be more likely sacrifices on the altar of efficient, economic purpose.

Even if we are to accept the axiom of economic definition, why assume it is necessarily age based? The real center of Lamm's argument is defended by Hastings Center ethicist Daniel Callahan. Sooner or later, he says, our means will be insufficient to cover our needs. At that time, the one function left for seniors, he suggests, will be to sacrifice themselves in the name of their inheritors. The reason is not economic but social. Youth is a good in and of itself: "What I believe ought to be the primary aspiration of the old . . . is to serve the young and the future."[16] Why? Well . . . it just is. And if that means seniors may die so that younger people get a greater share of our communal resources, well, why not? They've had their day.

"Who gets the care?" has been called an "intergenerational war" now being fought between different factions over whether to reward the past labors of senior citizens or invest in the future of children.[17] That the war may be real but its rationale wholly fictional is a possibility ignored by all but a few lonely scholars.[18] As the lives detailed in this book argue—and its final chapter suggests—ageism's simplistic assumptions—age equals cost without benefit; youth equals utility—are as baseless as they are generally accepted.

AGE AND THE "NATURAL" LIFE SPAN

There is, however, another problem with the arguments of Lamm, Callahan, and their supporters. Nobody can define with certainty the divisor between deserving youth and undeserving elders. How do we define the appropriate line between natural maturity and unnatural continuance? There is no "natural life span," one in which continuance is predestined. Most of us surviving to middle age have done so only with the help of various antibiotics, surgeries, and vaccines. Modernity's adults are, by definition, the beneficiaries of an unnatural science and advancing technology that have limited the traditionally vast cull of infants, children, adolescents, and younger adults naturally subject to the ravages of bacterial assault and viral attack.

Across the history of *homo sapiens*, few humans have lived long enough to enjoy the mixed pleasures of middle age, let alone extreme age. There is therefore no obvious biologic dateline dividing maturity from seniority. It is always a relative phenomenon, a cultural definition that shifts with the success of medical science and the determinations of society's leaders. Sometimes their assessments are accurate, sometimes not.[19] If the question is one of cost, wouldn't the healthy and active senior be more valuable than the infant with a congenital heart malformation whose continuance will require a risky heart transplant and lifelong medical attention?

THE LIVED LIFE

Academic theories offer little insight into the lived lives of individual seniors because few modern intellectuals concern themselves with individuals. Social gerontologists, psychologists, and ethicists of varying persuasions typically focus on the grand picture, the statistical pattern, or the class-based survey report. As a rule, they are not intimate with the people whose lives their work supposedly describes. Like the rest of us, most are too busy and too involved to take the time to know the senior who is the specific example of their professional concern. If a project needs individual questioning and contact, graduate research assistants are always available for the scut work few self-respecting scholars want to do themselves. And, I suspect, many of society's gerontologists and geriatricians enjoy the company of seniors no more than do the rest of us.

More to the point, academic careers are rarely made on the strength of detailed examinations of individual lives. Lucrative research projects, and the contracts for consultation that result from their conclusion, typically stem from the broad, anonymous survey, from census analysis and the structural portrait of a class or group. Given a cultural emphasis on utilitarian economic concerns, it is no surprise that data from these longitudinal studies most typically address issues of financial burden and cost-efficient care. The work returned, as Jaber F. Gubrium has argued eloquently, often says more about a researcher's goals, prejudices, and preconceptions than it does about the subjects of the research themselves.[20]

The inevitable result is theories that bear no necessary relation to the lives of the people they supposedly describe and policies that while theoretically sufficient do not respond to the needs of the citizens they supposedly serve. But a theory that does not answer the individual case is merely a prejudice dressed up as fact. A policy that does not speak to the needs of individuals is one whose only real beneficiary is the functionary or official. Because there is a broad, demographic pattern ($n = 1435$) does not mean it reflects the complex reality of a life lived over time within a specific community. A pattern may be accurately described yet wholly irrelevant to the lives of the people it supposedly delineates. We are, after all, both more and less than the sum of our biological cohorts. We are each a curious uniqueness of history and potential, of memory and of hopes embedded in a body that at any moment in our lives may be either frail or strong. To plan and predict on the bases of actuarial statistics and hoary assumptions divorced from experience is to assume a perfect world in which the lived life is necessarily ordered and constant; each moment lock-stepped in a progression that cannot be changed.

As an anecdote to the faceless theories of experts who reflexively dismiss the complex realities of the lives of the elderly, others have sought to collect the narratives of seniors themselves. The best of them—Studs Terkel's *Coming of Age*, for example—are richly impressionistic, useful for the occasionally telling anecdote or quote. Others have developed involved case histories, professional reports written from the perspective of the clinical researcher. Nobody does this better than Oliver Sacks, whose casebooks have raised the medical case review to the realm of high literature.[21]

The former, while stimulating, are rarely more than disparate collections whose individual voices raise questions the text itself never addresses. The latter, while often deep and insightful, represent a clinician's understanding of a patient's world. In both cases, tales told about or by this old man or that old woman remain little more than disparate, if tantalizing data. They are anecdotes chasing a theory. It is as if everyone sings his or her own song in a different tempo. The resulting cacophony cannot present a sustained and critical theme.

A CHORUS OF EXPERIENCE

This book seeks a middle course between the distinct paths of individual narrative and the broad lines of more general, social argument. It first presents the annotated life narratives of a series of seniors and then attempts to build from their narratives a picture of what it means to be elderly—over sixty-five years of age—in North American society. These are not full-blown, anthropologic histories, complete retellings of a lived life. Rather, they are the highlights of those lives—past and present—presented in the words and from the perspective of people who have experienced the events they relate. Each was asked to "Tell me your story," the famous welcoming words of Sigmund Freud to his clients. All were also asked—"Tell me about your life, today"—to match past and present together. No other directions were given. None, in the end, were needed.

This "chorus of experience"[22] provides an experiential base whose purpose from the start has been to evaluate the general assumptions of age and ageism—popular and academic—from the perspective of lived experience.

The first task, therefore, was to collect the assumptions and definitions of what age is and what it means to our society. The second was to build an experiential base of life narratives offered by those who are "old," sixty-five years of age at least, and who were willing to speak on the record about their lives. Finally, the two were joined in an attempt to weigh the assumptions we hold against lives as they are lived.

The experiences of the narrators, my co-authors, are the heart and soul of this exercise. It is the lives they have known—and remembered—that are the standard against which assumptions are weighed. These are not, however, "representative" seniors, people selected from a range of subjects because they fit a specific demographic profile. They are instead a heterogeneous collection whose salient, common characteristics are that all are over sixty-five years of age and all agreed to the interview process. Some are married, others are widowed or divorced. Most have lived their lives within the broad confines of North America's vast middle class, although some were at the low end of its socioeconomic range and others gained its upper rungs. Sherry Busch lives in public housing on a small pension and Social Security. Mrs. Bee, on the other hand, is a woman of considerable means. In 1988, Jake Epp's pensions and Social Security payments totaled almost $17,000. In that year Tina and Tim Harding's income from pension and investments was more than double that amount.

The very diversity these narrators present is, I submit, their greatest collective strength. We are given to speaking of the elderly as a homogeneous group. What characteristics do they share, however? Is there a common vision, a unity of experience and assumption that indeed gives seniors a single voice, a unanimity of position? If it makes human sense to define a group by their age, then it should make equal sense to use random members of that age group to examine the grand assumptions put forward for all who fall within that set. Simply, one sees what they have in common and where, person to person, their lives and perspectives differ.

Contrary to popular opinion, not all seniors are garrulous. There is no biological compulsion to bare one's soul after reaching sixty-five or seventy years of age. Some potential narrators refused a request for an interview on the basis of time—"I'm too busy"—or because they didn't feel comfortable with the process. My co-authors agreed to talk to me about their lives, and the important incidents in them, as a favor to a person most perceived as a friend. In the case of those who were merely acquaintances, I was welcomed as one at least sympathetic to and interested in their individual conditions. Relations with these narrators ranged from the distanced and formal to the familiar, depending on our histories and their preference.

Some insisted I refer to them by their Christian names, others preferred more formal reference. "Just call me Sherry," Mrs. Busch urged. This was not a simple sign of intimacy, although we were friends. It is instead the way she likes to be known by everyone from Ontario's lieutenant governor to the people she meets on the bus. Jake Epp, on the other hand, was always Mr. Epp to me.

In our conversations, I followed their suggestions, using first names with some, Mr. and Mrs. or Ms. with others. Here, too, I mix the formal and informal, especially in the postscripts to individual narratives. Because I want these narrators to be seen not as pleasant but inconsequential familiars, but as narrators with testimony worth considering, my tendency is to use respectful designations—"Mr. Epp" and "Mrs. Harding," for example, rather than "Jake" and "Tina." When this becomes tiresome I use full names—"Jake Epp" or "Tina Harding," for example—to assure that the falsely familiar "Jake" and "Tina" don't reflexively diminish their standing.

It is mostly as Mr. and Mrs. or Ms. that I think of them, however. It is how I was taught to refer to people older than myself. And while I am middle aged, that formality—I realize this as I'm writing it—is a mechanism that also distances me from their worlds and the points of commonality they share with mine. The very respect formality promises (I have tried for years to comfortably call my Aunt Janice by her first name, for example) simultaneously permits me to think of them as different and other, albeit in the nicest way.

The quality of data returned in these interviews is, I believe, more intimate and more revealing than it would be with a professional interviewer lacking any prior association to the speaker. In asking for their assistance, I explained my interests to each—"What does it mean to be old, today? How do you perceive this period of your life?"—and then made an appointment to record whatever observations and insights they wished to share. Once started, most spoke with little prompting, although of necessity their stories occasionally triggered the occasional question or comment from me when something was unclear.

If their narratives seemed to include a sometimes formidable cast of characters, I took this not as garrulous wandering but as proof that the world each inhabits is constructed not independently, but across layers of textured, historical association. "The person whom we describe, and over whom we theorize, is not the only agent in his world," R. D. Laing concluded in *Self and Others*. "How he perceives and acts towards the others, how they perceive and act towards him, how he perceives them as perceiving him, how they perceive him as perceiving them, are all aspects of 'the situation.' They are all pertinent to understanding a person's participation in it."[23]

This meant that the stories being told could not be prompted with pointed questions without losing the essentials of the narrative itself. "Directed interviews" that focus and limit the speaker's response—"Stay on point, please. That's not what we're talking about"—often say more about the researcher's interests than the subject's perceptions. And although I had a packet of questions I wanted answered—questions about their financial situation, current relations to younger family members, issues of life quality in age as opposed to life quality in younger maturity—these were introduced circumspectly, if at all, into these interviews.

Whatever my agenda, my companions knew what it was they wanted to say and were adroit in turning from my agenda to their own. "I realized quite early in this adventure that interviews, conventionally conducted, were meaningless," Studs Terkel once wrote in a passage I memorized years ago.[24] "The question-and-answer technique may be of value in determining favored detergents, toothpaste, and deodorants, but not in the discovery of men and women." And it was the discovery of these persons that I most wanted; the world from their eyes, the sense of it from their hearts.

My role, therefore, was that of a recorder and translator, first capturing on tape and then transposing into written form the experiences of my co-authors. Still, these tales are no less mediated for the fact of their taped capture. Like every translator and all recorders, my presence throughout these narratives is pervasive. These are human stories told to me, narratives in which I was an active audience whose reaction necessarily influenced the flow of the story itself. Afterwards, the text of each taped session was first edited to prune redundancies, then rearranged to assure that, in printed form, it reflected the flow and structure we expect of our literature.

Further, liberties have been taken to disguise the identities of individual speakers, all of whom have been given fictitious names. Several have been located, for the purposes of this work, in cities other than those in which they actually reside. Mr. Lamm never lived in Buffalo, New York, although his adult working life was lived in a city that resembles my hometown in many ways. The phone book for Toronto will show no Sherry Busch. A map of Ontario does not reveal a Toronto suburb named Billsley. This was necessary both for legal reasons—the publishers insisted—and to protect the anonymity of narrators whose frank statements about complex, personal situations would either open them to ridicule or offer unintended injury to other members of their interpersonal worlds.

In an attempt to understand these narratives, I began with the assumption that what each narrator presented was important, and if not a "true" interpretation of events—one subject to independent verification—one the narrator wholeheartedly believed. To do otherwise would have been to do violence to the perspectives presented and to the gifts of time and reminiscence these stories represent. As Robert Coles once cautioned, "One can interpret these statements, analyze them, work them into a social critique or criticism, but whatever use each of us may make of the words of others, they must be granted the possession of at least a 'glimmer of truth'—the deeply held convictions of men and women who are capable of fierce pride, shred realism, and insistent rejection of self-pity, or the pity of others, which can, of course, mask condescension or contempt."[25]

That sense of critical respect was, I like to think, my starting point. And so I have attempted to balance the affection I have for these narrators—and the enjoyment I have taken from their company—with the uses made in the last chapter of their narratives. My hope is that in reading these narratives my co-authors will see themselves not as foolish, frail oldsters whom life has passed by, but as I perceive them: People who possess a full measure of humanity and, perhaps, an insight or two that may inform the humanness we all seek.

SOCIAL ASSUMPTIONS

Opposed to the weight of their experience are the reflexive assumptions we as a society hold about the elderly. In the reading, it would be well to keep these in mind. First and foremost is the almost universally accepted proposition that the social lives of seniors (and thus their perceptions and expectations) are, by definition, qualitatively different from those of younger persons. Similarly, the life worlds of seniors are assumed to be necessarily distinct at their core from those of us who are "mature" but not elderly adults. Popular wisdom holds that most seniors (especially female seniors) are single, having outlived their spouses; overbearing in their presentation of boring nonsequiturs or silently locked into a realm of diseased memory; fragile of spirit and often grumpy.

They are either financial burdens draining family (and social) resources or profligate, greedy old goats spending the potential inheritances of younger folk. Further, seniors are reflexively assumed to be unproductive drags on the nation's social and economic body, a group contributing little to the commonweal. Finally, implicit in most perspectives on aging and gerontology is the assumption that, whatever a senior's health status, he or she has no sense of a future, no anticipation of new experiences or the joyous potential of tomorrow.

At one time we believed longevity led to wisdom, and thus that the wisest people among us were necessarily also the oldest. The wealth of their accumulated experience was a repository of data—about the environment or a shared history—that could be accessed in no other way. This was the view of traditional cultures, of the native peoples of North America and of cultures like those of the Chinese and the Japanese. Wisdom is the one virtue modern experts cede to the old, what Erik Erikson termed a "basic strength" of the age group.[26] But in modernity's world of books, records, tapes, cinema, and television, this once common assumption has given way to the suspicion that seniors are probably foolish, a tad childish, and possessed of a body of wisdom that will not serve in today's advancing postmodern, millennial world. Thus, the stories seniors tell are popularly assumed to be tedious or, at best, irrelevant anecdotes of a time long past.

In the same vein, many assume that age is defined by diminished faculties, that a foolish forgetfulness is the necessary companion of continuance. In the late twentieth century, we have made of Alzheimer's, the disease of forgetfulness, a definition of age. Never mind that all seniors do not become forgetful or that dementing conditions—of which Alzheimer's is only one—can strike people in their thirties, forties, fifties, or sixties. Forget those who are in their seventies and eighties who write books and articles, perform music, or care for their grandchildren. We assume that the aged are different because they forget and in their forgetting become nonpersons who give up their place in our world.

Finally, we assume that seniority's difference lies, at least in part, in its being the end stage of life. The elderly are presumably prone to what some call "disengagement" because they are frail and preparing to die. It is believed to be both natural and inevitable that those whose lives are almost ended will tidy up, withdraw, and review what has gone before. What remains unclear, however, is whether "disengagement" is a common consequence of longevity and, if so, whether it results from having lived overlong or is born of the social restrictions imposed on the elderly. "There can be little doubt that today the discontinuity of family life as a result of dislocation contributes greatly to the lack in old age of that minimum of vital involvement that is necessary for staying alive," Erikson wrote in the 1980s. "And lack of vital involvement often seems to be the nostalgic theme hidden in the overt symptoms that bring old people to psychotherapy."[27] In other words, perhaps what we see as the natural withdrawal of seniors may result not from a natural process but from their general abandonment. Perhaps we have made them into isolates, deprived them of everything *but* a featureless present in which all they have is a review of their past. If that is true, it indicts us all.

It is this type of questioning these narratives will hopefully provoke. In their reading, the first question is whether the lives described are truly different from those we younger people live and, if so, is that difference a function of age alone? If they are different, is it because the narrators are wise or foolish, filled with humanity, or embittered by Erikson's disdain? Are these people a burden and, if so, is that burden unique to age or defined by something else? Finally, the question will be whether the differences found across these narratives result from age's disabilities and strengths or are they the inevitable consequence of a social isolation we have, perhaps, forced on those seniors who still reside uneasily in our midst?

NOTES

1. Joseph Heller, *God Knows* (New York: Dell, 1989; reprinted Scribners, 1997).

2. Simone de Beauvoir, *The Coming of Age* (New York: Putnam and Sons, 1972), 239.

3. Tom Koch, "No More Christmas Cookies," in *A Place in Time: Care Givers for Their Elderly* (New York: Praeger, 1993), 127–136.

4. Michelle Locke, Tired Kin Opting to "Dump Granny," *Raleigh News & Observer*, November 28, 1991, B3.

5. Tamara K. Haraven, The Last Stage: Historical Adulthood and Old Age, *Daedalus* (1976): 105.

6. Leon Trotsky, *Trotsky's Diary in Exile*, Trans. Elena Zarudnaya (Cambridge, MA: Harvard University Press, 1976).

7. M. J. Malinowski, Capitation, Advances in Medical Technology, and the Advent of a New Era in Medical Ethics, *American Journal of Law and Medicine* 22, nos. 2&3 (1996): 341.

8. Erik H. Erikson, *The Life Cycle Completed* (New York: W. W. Norton, 1982), 62.

9. These are phrases used in *Time* magazine and other popular periodicals whose headline writers seek to set the general political and social tone of an article.

10. For a recent and surprisingly sympathetic comment on Lamm's ageist arguments, see David C. Thomasma, Stewardship of the Aged: Meeting the Ethical Challenge of Ageism, *Cambridge Quarterly of Healthcare Ethics* 8, no. 1 (1999): 148–150.

11. Daniel Callahan, *Setting Limits: Medical Goals in an Aging Society* (New York: Simon & Schuster, 1987.

12. Tamara Haraven, The Last Stage: Historical Adulthood and Old Age, *Daedalus* 105 (1976): 14.

13. Karl T. Riabowol, Editorial: Basic Biological Aging Research in Canada: Time for Rejuvenation? *Canadian Journal on Aging* 15, no. 1 (1996): 1–4.

14. David P. Barash, *Aging: An Exploration* (Seattle: University of Washington Press, 1983).

15. "The ten commandments of an aging society" were pronounced as a policy speech to the Eddy foundation in New York. For a discussion of Lamm's assumption that the young will suffer if seniors are maintained, see R. Hoopes, When It's Time To Leave; Can Society Set an Age Limit for Health Care? *Modern Maturity* 31 (1988): 38–43. For a more recent view, see David C. Thomasma, Stewardship of the Aged: Meeting the Ethical Challenge of Ageism, *Cambridge Quarterly of Healthcare Ethics* 8, no. 2 (1999): 148–159.

16. Daniel Callahan, *Setting Limits: Medical Goals in an Aging Society* (New York: Simon & Schuster, 1987), 43.

17. See, for example, Alanna Mitchell, Seniors Gain at Expense of Young, Report Says, *Globe and Mail*, July 15, 1992, A7.

18. Elizabeth A. Binney and Carroll L. Estes, The Retreat of the State and Its Transfer of Responsibility, *International Journal of the Health Sciences* 19, no. 1 (1988): 83–96.

19. For a review of the creation of aging as an academic discipline, see Stephen Katz, *Disciplining Old Age: The Formation of Gerontological Knowledge* (Charlottesville: University of Virginia Press, 1996).

20. Jaber F. Gubrium, Voice, Context, and Narrative in Aging Research, *Canadian Journal on Aging* 14, no. 1 (1995): 68–81.

21. In his search for the boundaries of humanness, Sacks has included several cases involving seniors, with descriptions of Parkinson's, auditory hallucinations, and the disinhibitions of tertiary syphilis. See Oliver Sacks, *The Man Who Mistook His Wife for a Hat* (New York: Summit Books, 1985).

22. Tom Koch, *Watersheds: Stories of Crisis and Renewal in Our Everyday Life.* (Toronto: Lester Publishing, 1994). Revised edition issued as *Second Chances: Crisis and Renewal in Our Everyday Lives.* (Toronto: turnerbooks, 1998).

23. R. D. Laing, *Self and Others* (New York: Penguin Books, 1969), 82.

24. Studs Terkel, *Division Street: America* (New York: Avon Books, 1967), prefatory notes.

25. Robert Coles, Work and Self-respect, *Daedalus* 105 (1976): 37.

26. Erik Erikson, *The Life Cycle Completed* (New York: W. W. Norton, 1982), 33.

27. Ibid., 63.

1

A Brocaded Brassiere with Red Knickers

What's in a man's age? He must hurry more, that's all; cram in a day what his youth took a year to hold.
Henry W. Longfellow, 1877

For more than forty years, Sherry Busch has been the moving force behind a series of programs for seniors in the Toronto area. Beginning as an employee of the city's parks and recreation program, she remains an activist for fragile seniors now her contemporaries. The recipient of numerous awards, she currently supervises, in a volunteer capacity, a summer parks program in East Toronto that hosts seniors from regional nursing homes as well as the immediate neighborhood. We first met in 1990 and have been friends ever since, getting together occasionally for coffee and the gossip we both enjoy.

One medical note is required as a preface to her story. In it she is at pains to point out that her biliary cirrhosis is "not from drinking." In this she is correct. It is a liver disease occurring when bile improperly processed by the liver seeps into the skin, causing, among other symptoms, intolerable and constant itching. Its cause is unrelated to alcoholism.

Some of us are afraid to die, very much afraid to die. My own mother didn't want to die. She was the best woman who ever stepped on two feet. Whether she was afraid of the Other Side or she just didn't want to leave us, I'll never know. But I do know my mom didn't want to die. My dad, he didn't give a darn. He said to me, "Oh, there's adventure on the

Other Side too, you know." So I didn't feel so bad when my dad passed away. But when Mother went, I did feel bad about it. I have to admit it. But it was a lesson to me, and I could pass that on to other seniors.

We all know that we're at the top of the hill and we're sliding down the other side. All of us seniors. I find that I'm not on the ball the way I used to be. I used to stand up and talk for two or three hours and never repeat myself and could always find the word I needed. Can't do that today, and I know that. When I was really lively and full of pep, I could go like the dickens all day long and all night, too. But gradually, you see, it began to take its toll. And gradually I realized I was getting older and my body was getting older and that I would have to do something about it.

Yes, I felt it, and you can't help but know it. I mean, you go through all those things and you know damn well they're taking their toll. I've told a lot of people that my electrolytes have gone out, which is quite true. Is it frustrating? Yes, unless I think, "Oh, you damn fool. For Pete's sake, smarten up. You're getting old. It's going to happen, so face it." And I go on to something else. I was thinking, "Gee, am I going to sit down and let this take over, or am I going to fight it every step of the way?" I'm still fighting. And there are so many seniors I've helped by doing that.

The only thing I get mad at when I look in the mirror is the wrinkles. Geez, I get mad at that. But I think, "Oh, what the hell. Just call them 'laughing wrinkles,' and go ahead." I went back to my chiropractor, who's really shy and a real good guy. I had to take my slacks off, naturally, and he said, "That's all, Sherry, just your slacks. You don't need to take off anything else." And I said, "There isn't a hell of a lot left underneath the slacks, anyway." So he kind of shook his head, and I said, "Oh, don't you peek at my bum, because it looks like a venetian blind at my age." Well, he just about went through his skull. "Oh, Sherry," he said, "you're terrible. Sherry, you're awful."

Anytime I have something wrong with me, I always make a joke of it. I always make somebody laugh because of it. Even when I tell them all about this doctor having to go in twice to get a hunk of my liver to analyze. I'll say: "I just told her, 'Hold it, Hold it! Don't put it in that jar, I want to see it.' And she said, 'Oh, Mrs. Busch, you don't want to see it!' And I said, 'Look, it's my insides you're taking out. I want to see it.' "

I've had biliary cirrhosis of the liver—and it's not from drink or rich food. And then I had a cancer operation. All sorts of other things happened to me. The accident [a fall] that I had, and gout with my legs, and like that. And I thought, well, there's only one thing that you can do, and that's climb over the top of it. Now I'm not going to go around and tell everybody my troubles, but if they ask me what I've got, I'm going to find some way to make a joke about it. So many a time I've said, "Oh, geez, I'd rather be pregnant. At least I'd have the memory. But, by God, you can't hold gout in your arms, and you're not going to kiss the thing!" Sometimes I'll say to them, "Well, you know what's wrong with me?" Then I'll say, "Well, hell, I haven't had so much as a wink [sex] in fifteen years!" And they'll say, the seniors, "Oh, Sherry, you're terrible! You're awful." But they think it's funny.

I've had two crooked arms all my life. My right arm is deformed because of the bone structure, and my left arm is deformed because it was broken in three places when I was three years old and they couldn't set it properly. But I'm not complaining. I've had a lot of fun with them. When I went to school, and I did calisthenics, everyone would get behind me just to see my crooked arms. My teacher at school said the doctors had told them that my arm was in very bad condition and to be very careful of me, not to let me run or carry on or anything. So, if they were doing something that I didn't like, I'd say, "Oohh, aahh," and the teacher would say, "Sherry, does your arm ache?" And I'd say, "No, no, I'm all right. I'm sorry, I didn't mean to disturb things." "Now, Sherry," the teacher would say, "get right over there by that radiator, and you get that heat on your arm." Oh, I used it, I used it so many times. And sometimes I think that just doing that as a child helped me so much through life.

Now if I wanted to sit down and tell everybody all the aches and pains I've had, and the worries I've had, I could bore the life out of them. For example, I had three husbands. My first husband was in the U.S. Army, and he got it at Guam. My other two husbands, they thought it was wonderful, my work with seniors and how much I looked after them, and they loved the seniors as much as I did.

I only had one son, and he was in the navy. Bill, my first husband, was the only boy with four sisters. On my side, there were only two of us, my brother and me. So to have a baby boy in the family, that was great. Well then, when my son was only forty-three, he passed away with a terrible heart attack. My other two husbands have died too. So, really, the only thing I had left was the seniors. Everything outside of looking after my husbands was for my seniors.

I'm seventy-seven and feel thirty-seven and, sometimes, act seventeen. But that's just for the benefit of my seniors because they like it when I act the nut. Goodness gracious, there's enough of them! Last year, at this very program right here, we had 3,780 senior citizens from hospitals, from homes, and what we call the "walk-ins." They're the people who have their own home and are able to walk or take the streetcar. I drive, but I don't have that far to come. Since I had the silly gout, I've been very much afraid to drive too far because sometimes I get these terrific pains in my legs, and thank goodness it's in the left leg, since my car is automatic. But still, I'm afraid I'm going to hurt someone else or hurt myself. So I don't drive too far but, as it is, I don't live more than a quarter mile from here, on the lake [*Lake Ontario*]. Beautiful.

I've been working with them for years. Oh, for a long time, long before I became a senior myself. I was with the Department of Parks and Recreation, and they asked me if I would take over an adult class. I was working for them, getting good money, too. At first, I worked with the children, but then they needed someone a little bit older with a little more experience to do the adult classes. That was just great, but they also gave me a senior citizens' class, which was out at Regent Park. When they were stuck at Regent Park for somebody to take over, this one supervisor said to me, "Sherry, these are all very nice people. You can't be as rough and tough with them as you are with the ladies in your adult classes." So I said, "Well, then, what did you ask me for? You've got lots of other employees you can ask." "Well," she said, "I don't think there's anyone who can handle them like you can." She said, "Now, it's only going to be until after Christmas, so try and behave yourself." So that's all she had to say to me, and I thought, "Boy, I'm going to fix this."

Well, I got so sick and tired of just playing Pass the Parcel and silly little games. It broke my heart to think that seniors were subjected to that kind of childish stuff. So I got the Department of Parks to help me, and I got the [*Regent Park community*] residents to help me, and we got instruments, and I had a band. More of a review than a band, thirty-six people in it. I even had a striptease. Yeah, she was seventy-six! After she stripped, she had more on her than when she started. Oh, that went over big, I tell you. Everybody let out a shriek because I had Velcro on the back of her dress, you see. She sang "All of me, why not take all of me?" At the end, she put her arms up and sang out, "Why not take all of me?" and, as she said it, I pulled these strings on the back of her dress and it fell off. It was a beautiful brocaded dress—but no straps. I brocaded her brassiere to make it look like the straps of the dress, you see. Then underneath her dress she had these fiery red satin knickers with about six inches of gold lace on the bottom. When the dress fell off her, oh! The whole place just shrieked. And I don't think there was ever a night that somebody didn't come and say, "I felt so sorry for that lady when her dress fell off."

I tell you when I got them in that band, when I got them all going, that supervisor nearly had a fit. Oh, my God! Terrible. And yet, the Commissioner [of Parks] thought it was marvelous. From that time on, I enjoyed the seniors so much that I started working with them. "Treat them like ladies," she said. But they don't want to be treated that way. They want to be treated the way I treat them, full of hell. Let's go back to the way we were when we used to be able to do this, that, and the other thing, I say.

The other day we had The Singing Policemen [*from the Toronto Police Band*] here in the park. You don't call them that anymore. You call them, "The Badge." They came and, oh, the music was marvelous. Gout or no, I had to dance! I couldn't help it. So I had them in their wheelchairs and grabbed their little old hands, and I had them going, dancing with their hands. And some of them said, "Oh, I can't do that! Oh, don't touch me. I can't do that." I said, "Give me your hands. Here, course you can. I'm going to whack your butt if you talk to me like that." And sure enough, I'm shaking their hands, moving them in time to the music, and the first thing I know is I get laughs and giggles all over the place. That's all you need to do. Just show that you love them.

You've seen me with the seniors down here—I never get on that bus to say good-bye to them but I don't say, "Now everybody shut up for a minute." And everybody looks up and I'll say, "You all being quiet?" And they'll say yes. "All right," I say, "listen to me. I love you." And they'll say, "Oh, Sherry, we love you too." God, that's all you need, somebody to come out and say, "I love you." They come for the program, but I think they come for the love. They can't come here and not feel it. Every year I've had a staff and they have been wonderful. Of course, this is something they're trained for. Before they even come on this job, we have at least three days when they're trained about what's expected of them. They're good to the seniors. And this is why the seniors come here. They must be able to feel the love, to feel the feeling that we have for them.

There are some bitchy seniors. Yep. Some real bitchy seniors. And I just look at them, the ones who are the bitches, their mouths are drooping. The ones who are good sports, who come here for a good time—who'll do any little thing for anybody—they're the ones where you see the corners of their mouths turn up. We have one woman here who, well, nothing would please her. If the Lord himself came down to serve her coffee, she'd say, "You put too much cream in it." But I don't know. I can't look back into her younger life. I don't know who hurt her. I don't know whether she didn't have a happy childhood. I don't know what made her like that. There has to be a reason for it. And yet, she comes every day and sits by herself. I can't figure it out.

They're very much afraid of being hurt. They're so afraid of being handicapped, more than what they are, because they've been able to handle it; probably for two or three years they've been about the same. They've got to the point where they could handle it. Now they're terrified that if they get up off that chair or if they don't have this to support them or that to support them, they could easily hurt themselves and they'd be worse off than before. So it does frighten them. It makes it hard to work with them. Even my daughter-in-law. She's in the hospital right now. She's a bit older than my son was, and she's only maybe fifteen years younger than I am. She said she was very much afraid that her son from another marriage would take the car keys away from her because, she said, "I am getting a pacemaker, Sherry." And I said, "Well, if you are getting a pacemaker, it's supposed to do you all the good in the world. You're supposed to be smartened up and be able to do all these things." And I told her, "If I were you, I'd have the doctor talk to him and tell him that this is why you're getting it. That he should have taken the keys from you *before* the pacemaker."

Over at a church on Ward Island [*an island in Lake Ontario connected to Toronto by ferry service*], they asked if I would go around Regent Park and find any seniors who were stuck in one room in their family home, find out if their children ever took them out on the weekend, if they ever took them to a show or anything. See if they would like to come to the church program. If they, the seniors, wanted to come to the program, it would cost them a streetcar ticket to get down to the boat, and a streetcar ticket to get over to the island. From there on, they'd be taken care of. Do you know that out of the whole of Regent Park, I found only two seniors who were willing to come out of that back room? That's out of, I would say, 120 people! I must have visited ten a day.

It seemed to me the seniors did not want to come out. Maybe I'm wrong about this, but I got the feeling that the majority of seniors were afraid that their families would get mad at them if they came out. Now that's the feeling I got, and several other ladies who were working with me, we sat down and talked about it and they had the same feeling: that these seniors were afraid to come out. You know, some families can be awful cruel to their people. I'm talking about mentally and physically. Absolutely. Being punished, that's the feeling that I got. That they were being punished for something and they had no idea what they had done. Just that they were old, that's why they were being punished. That's the feeling I got.

You see, nine times out of ten, when the senior goes in with the family, they have young children there. Or babies, even. And some seniors just can't stand the noise of those kids. Can't stand the sauciness of them. And, of course, some of them will be nasty to the kids. And, of course, the parents of the kids get peeved about it. And they're crabbin' about it: she did this, he did this, she did that. What are we going to do about it?

Not everyone, of course. Some of them are not stuffed into one room. They're allowed the run of the house. There are a lot of places the mother or the father have been taken such good care of. Oh, definitely. They never go out unless they ask if he doesn't want to come along. Or does she want to come along. And a lot of them are really good to their parents. Thank God for that. But it's always that bad apple in the barrel that messes things up.

The most important thing to me is keeping them in their own home. You know, I've heard a lot of people saying the same thing: "I believe in having them in their own home. But they've got to be supervised." Probably they do need a bit of help. I would suggest that they be very, very careful with stoves, for example. I had a sweetheart in my apartment, a lady I looked after sometimes—I'd take her to get her hair done. Bless her heart, she was in her nineties. But one day, she left all the jets on, on the stove, and she came out screaming, "Sherry, I can't get them off, I can't get them off." If she hadn't come screaming for me, there could have been a fire. Now there's enough people, God knows, out of work, that at least we could have them coming in, say, for two hours in the morning, maybe go to somebody else for two hours, and come back to look after her for two hours in the afternoon. There's no reason we can't. But what we have here instead is the buddy system where we watch out for each other.

Oh, the buddy system is just great. A lot of seniors would rather have that than their families phoning them because their families always have something to crab about or ask for. But with the buddy system, they know everybody is on the same level. People are neighbors and they look after each other. They've even got sheets, now, that are all made out with everyone's telephone number. Ontario Housing has done that.

I must have, gosh, four names that I call every day. So when they get up in the morning—and they know I'm up at six o'clock—they'll phone and say, "I slept good last night, Sherry. I feel fine today. How about you?" And I'll say, "I feel good, I'm off to the park." Or, if you can find somebody of the opposite sex, what the heck? I have no idea how old you have to be to lose your yen for sex. I don't know. But if they feel like it, what the hell's wrong with it? Love covers a whole lot of things. Friendship covers a whole lot of things.

This little soul I was telling you about, you know, who turned the stove on? They never told me, but they took her and they put her in a home. She was there two weeks and she died. You see, they didn't go to see her. She was in a completely strange place. She pined away. She wanted her home, she wanted her family, and they just didn't go. She wanted her friends, but nobody knew she was there. They didn't tell me! No. Oh, I felt terrible about that, because they knew I looked after her. Who else would do it, for heaven's sake? Some people, they just want to go their own way. I think they forget just exactly what their mum or their dad did for them when they were younger.

NURSING HOMES

Do people go into nursing homes because they need help or because their families want them to? Both, both. If they want to get rid of them, they'll get a doctor's certificate and put them in a home. That's it. Get rid of them! Everything the poor old soul owns gets signed over to the kids and they put them in a home. And that's it. Maybe they'll go once a week to see them. So a lot of them are heartbroken. A lot of them are heartbroken because they expected when they got to be a certain age, their families would take care of them. Or there would still be the love there. If they had to go into a home, then they expected the family would come to them.

There isn't an awful lot to tell, just a heartache. When some of them come to me, or ask me to go to them, they say to me, "What am I going to do, Sherry? They said they would take me in and look after me, so I sold my house. Now they want to put me into a home." I tell them it's a law that if you sold your house and they're putting you in a home, they've got to pay a certain amount. You can use your old-age pension, yes. But they'll have to declare how much you got for the house if they're going to take their share of it. Still, it's a rotten thing to do.

You see, in their own home, they're in their own surroundings. They know where this is, they know where that is. But if you take them out of their own home and put them in a place they know nothing whatsoever about, they've lost all their surroundings. And, you see, when you put them in a home, there's only three or four people taking care of a whole mess of them. They don't have the time to do it! So the seniors just sit there. I mean, they turn on television, but it's not what they want. And I've never yet seen an attendant take a look up and see if there was something worthwhile on that television. Never. They say, "There's your television. Watch that!" What the hell is there on television for the seniors to watch? There isn't anything.

How many people go into a nursing home to sit and talk with them for an hour? How many people will go into a nursing home and be jolly with them, tell them jokes or something silly about themselves? If they go in to visit them in a nursing home, it's "Oh, you poor dear! Look at that one over there. Isn't she in an awful mess?" I mean, they're pointing out all the terrible things that are going on rather than really and truly making it a happy visit for them. I've noticed it so many, many times. I mean, there's many a time something nice will be on television, some kind of music or something, and I'll say, "Come on, let's all dance." And I'm up there in the middle, acting the fool, and they think that's wonderful. They really do.

I don't hide my religion. I don't hide my feelings. Would I say I'm pleased to be Christian? I'm so pleased to be me! I'm so pleased that in my lifetime I had a mother and father who were very good people, extremely good people. My mother was a wonderful woman. My father was the greatest old reprobate that ever stepped on two feet. He was captain on the waters. Bless his heart, he was a great old guy. He was a great man. So I was blessed with good parents. And I think through this I've carried it all through my life.

I stayed with my mother for thirteen years. She was ninety-nine when she passed away. Now, Mum had arthritis, naturally, at her age. She had a cancer operation at ninety. Up until that time, when I had the band at Regent Park, my mother played second drum. Of course, she played it as if she was afraid she was going to hurt the drum. But she still played it. And she looked forward to going, and this was well into her eighties. My poor mother, she used to say, "Sherry, I have no idea why in the world I married your father." Dad was a sea captain, away a lot. And I'd say, "To get someone like me." And she'd say, "Well, you've got a point with that."

It was just the love that we had for one another. I mean, gosh, I lost three husbands, and that didn't mean as much to me as when I lost my mum. There was such a bond between us. As a child, my mother had been so good. One thing I can always remember was how good she was to her own mother and how good she was to her father's mother. I've always remembered that, and how I was taught to respect my grandparents. And how dearly I loved them. My mother looked after them—both of them. They died right in my mother's arms and her own father died right in her arms. And mother practically died in my arms. It was Sunday morning, and I knew she was going, and I knew she didn't want to go.

When Mum broke her hip and I had my accidents, everybody said, "Sherry, you'll have to put Nanny in a home." Well, of course, I was associated with all the homes and I knew everybody and that. And I thought, well, that's fine, if I do put my mother in a home, it's not permanent. I knew that if I put her there just until I got back on my feet, everything would be just fine. So I did. I put her in a nursing home. Just for some relief for me, until I got back on my feet. Well, I couldn't stand it after nineteen days. It broke my heart to see those poor souls sitting there and all they had to look forward to were meals. You'd see them sitting, waiting for the next meal, you know? Oh, God, it was awful. She never complained. My mother never complained about a thing. Finally I said, "Mum, would you come home with me?"

By this time, you see, Mum was just a little bit out on cloud nine somewhere. And her very good friend when she was young—they went to school together and they were each other's bridesmaids—her name was Mabel. After Mum had her operation, her cancer operation, I was no longer her daughter. I was her girlfriend, Mabel. So she said she never could understand why I called her "Mum." Why did I call her Mum? And I said, "It's just a habit with me. You just have to put up with it. I'm a nut, and that's all there is to it."

Of course, after she had the cancer operation, she couldn't take care of herself anymore, but I brought her home with me. And the minute she walked inside the door she said, "Oh, Mabel, we're back home again." Uh huh. But, I mean, even though I was her girlfriend—I was no longer her daughter—she still knew where her bedroom was. She knew where the bathroom was. She knew enough to say, "Mabel, get me a drink of water." Or, "Mabel, is it time for my pill?" She was coherent, there were no two ways about it. Lots of little things she couldn't remember from day to day, but way back, she could remember. Oh, yeah. As long as Mum was there, as long as she recognized me as something in her life, oh, I was happy as the dickens.

Myself, I had to have a biopsy for the liver, which is grim, positively grim. It's like them taking an Italian stiletto and just sticking it in. And of course all they can do is freeze the skin. They can't freeze you in the center. Whew! I wouldn't want to go through that again. And when I had to go to hospital, the doctor who did it there, she had to go in a second time, right after the first one. And she wasn't very nice. She kept saying, "Mrs. Busch, you've got to straighten that arm. You've got to." And I was doing the very best that I could. Finally, I said to her, "Look here, let's just stop this nonsense for one minute. I want to show you something." And she said, "Hmm, I really haven't the time. I have other patients." And I said, "Not right now, you haven't. You've got me." And I said, "You'll listen to what I have to say. Both my arms are deformed, and I can't straighten them."

That's when they found out that I had biliary cirrhosis. I mean, that's it. Right in her office the doctor said, "You know, you're such a strong-willed person. You're the type of person we would like to try this transplant treatment on." Truthfully speaking, I think they only wanted to experiment with me. I really, truly do. And I thought to myself, at my age they're going to waste somebody's liver? They could give it to a younger person. They'd have years to live! I've only got, if I'm lucky, another twenty years to go. But with the way things are going today, maybe I'm not so lucky. So right there and then, she phoned the London Hospital and she could not get hold of the doctor she's associated with. So she said, "I'll phone you tomorrow, Mrs. Busch, and we'll make arrangements." And I said, "Don't bother, because I'm not going to do it." "Oh, well," she said. "You'd be just perfect for it." And I said, "I don't care if I am or not, you find someone else that's more perfect than I am."

I think they were experimenting on me! I couldn't see depriving some young person of a life! I mean, I'd had a pretty doggone good life myself, and I expected to have a little bit more. Even if I had only three, four years to go, I could get something out of it. Or give something. That transplant liver for me would have been a waste. I can't see wasting anything. I can't see wasting time. And I can't see wasting food. And to waste a perfectly good liver on me! How did they know it was going to take? It was an experiment. No! The person who gave that liver, didn't he have the right to have it put into someone younger so it would last a little longer? I honestly think that. If I haven't lived a good life and done the deeds I should have done by now, I'm never going to do them! But a younger person has a chance of doing something for this world. And we need it, badly. So if it's a decision between me getting it or them, I'd definitely say, "Give it to the younger person. Providing they're a good person." You don't know, of course, but you've got to take your chances. You've got to. I mean, how many times have we made the wrong choice?

REFLECTIONS

I look at myself and think, boy, the life that's behind me. You know, there's not many people who have had the life I've had. I could just sit right down and write the most interesting book. In fact, I could write volumes. But no, I'm very happy with the way my life has been. Right now, I don't think I'd want to give up my privacy. I have a nice apartment, a lovely apartment with Ontario Housing. It's in a little building—only forty-three apartments—and I overlook the lake, which is my love. I do love the water, and especially that lake. And I can see all the way from the Summerville Pool to the CN Tower downtown. So you see, I'm lucky there. I've got that apartment because of my work with seniors.

The Department of Parks is very, very kind to me. I mean, I don't get paid for my work or anything, but they'll put up with my nonsense. Even the Commissioner of Parks will say, "Oh, my God, here comes Sherry. She wants something." He teases me, and he's a fine chap. The last time I was in the hospital, they sent me a beautiful plant. It's almost a tree. For Pete's sake, if it gets any larger, I'm going to have to cut a hole into my neighbor's apartment upstairs. It's things like that, that people do for me—so unexpected. Such kindnesses, such friendship given to me. In my later years, I have found more friendship, more genuine friendship, than in my whole life put together.

Family? My nieces and nephews, great-nieces and great-nephews. They drive me crazy, God love 'em. My niece's husband walked out on her and she had a lot of bills to pay, so she asked me if she could borrow my Visa card. And Sherry was fool enough to let her have it. When I got the bill, it was $1,500, and I have no idea how she's going to pay me back. Not unless she takes him back until the bill's paid and then throws him out again. Her husband's a high-rigger and he gets a fantastic wage.

Her daughter, my great-niece, it's all the same to her. My niece wasn't married to this chap, and they had this little girl, eight years old now. They paid $800 a month for that apartment, and he had to support this other boy by another marriage, and I think he had to pay the rent for his former wife. That meant my niece had to go out to work. And then one time, he just packed his bags and left. And I thought a lot of him, I really did. I liked him very much. Now, she's trying to get on welfare, and her lawyer says she can make sure the guy pays support, but, in the meantime, what do you do?

I lent $10,000 to her and this chap to get established. That was in 1985, and I've had $900 paid back since. I knew by the tone of her voice when she phoned last night that she wanted some money. So I said, "Gee, I'm awfully worried. I wish I had never let you have my Visa card. There's several things that I wanted, and I can't have them because I haven't got my Visa card." Anything to keep us away from the subject.

But she said, "You know it's Marilee's birthday at the end of August, and there's a beautiful outfit. . . . Oh, Auntie Sherry, I know how you like to see her beautifully dressed. And I wanted to get her this outfit for her birthday." So I said, "Is it expensive?" And she said, "Well, no, not for what you have to pay for kids' clothes today." And I asked how much it was, and she said $80, and I said, "Glory be to God! The kid's only eight years old. That's twice what I spend on myself." And she said, "Well, it's different for you, Auntie Sherry. You can buy anything, and you can alter it." And I said, "Well, give me a couple of weeks and I'll make something for her, and it won't cost any $80." Holy crow! Kids' clothes are expensive, but not like that, especially when she's in that kind of spot.

Oh, God, I've got to get my Visa card back. I can't let her run up anything more. And the thing is, I'm going to have to pay that $1,500, because I don't want my credit hurt. She's going to run it up and, if she doesn't pay it, think of the interest they'll put on it. I said to her, "I'll pay the $1,500, but give me back my card." And she said, "Oh, Auntie Sherry, let me pay it. Give me the responsibility, please." I said, "You've had the responsibility all along." I'm waiting to see what's on it this month when it comes in.

I figured they were going to get it when I died anyways because I have nobody close to me at all. You see, I lost my son when he was only forty-three. They're my only family. The thing is, I don't mind giving them money, but I can't stand getting into debt with the Visa card. I've never had a debt in my life, and I don't want to start now. If anyone had ever told me that I'd have that much money to hand out to my family, I wouldn't have believed it. Used to be that five or ten bucks was a lot of money. But I didn't mind handing that out to them.

My husbands left me pretty well off, and I had a great time traveling as far as I could go in the world. Then I figured I might just as well let them have some of it because they're going to get it anyways. But darn it all, it would be nice to have a bit of it while I'm still here. I don't know, maybe I'll live as long as my mum did. After all, she was ninety-nine when she died. And then who will look after me? What's the moral of the story? Give them little bits, but not great big bits. And never, never lend them your Visa card.

POSTSCRIPT

On the one hand, Sherry Busch speaks frankly of her own age, of the physical and emotional changes that accompany her seventy-seven years. She has, after all, buried three husbands and a son; she has suffered serious physical ailments and, in the mirror, sees the wrinkles and the diminution that have transformed her physically into an old woman. And yet, she insists that although seventy-seven years old at the time of this interview, she "feels thirty-seven and acts seventeen." It is posturing she clearly enjoys, although she says she does it for her clients because "they like it when I play the fool."

But in fact there is little that is foolish about Sherry Busch. It is hard to describe the mixture of fragility and energy that this small, extremely thin, extremely determined woman projects. When music plays—and at the summer program there is always music playing—she *has* to dance. She will cha-cha or rumba up to a solitary, wheelchair-bound individual, grab his (or her) hands, and dance with or at them despite the protests that inevitably accompany such a meeting. It is as if by her activity and determination she can hold their frailties at bay while imbuing her own energy and zest, through movement, to a partner.

The summer program employees are college-age students who both admire her and worry that Sherry's health will fail. They and several of the more regular seniors who attend the park meetings are perennially concerned that she will exhaust her physical resources. Each summer day at the park is a dance between Sherry's desire to do and the insistence of others that she sit, relax, and amuse herself by supervising the paid employees who knew precisely what had to be done. It is a touching and surprisingly intimate exchange to watch, their concern for her reflecting her concern for others; Sherry's desire to be able and their conviction that she is at least as fragile as many of the other, senior clients.

Sherry Busch personifies the ideal of active if fragile age, and perhaps more generally of the shared if fragile life, irrespective of age. She is not immune to the ailments and doubts that attend other seniors living with physical frailties and limits. But, for her, these are catalogued, acknowledged, and dismissed because, to Sherry, life as a senior citizen—like life at any age—is to be enjoyed to the fullest. In 1997, for example, she was studying, teaching, or performing yoga, mime, calligraphy, and puppetry at one or another senior center. It usually required two weeks' notice before she could find time on her calendar to make an appointment for our coffee hour.

Over the years of our acquaintance, her studies and work have been interrupted periodically by illnesses and physical problems. For her, continuance is an ongoing compromise between physical limits and determined desire. This is discussed indirectly in her concern for money, the balancing between her savings as "future legacy" and as a bulwark against fragile need. As with others, finances are for her a metaphor for a range of intergenerational tensions.[1] Sherry sees what she has saved as a potential inheritance for loved ones who will live after her and a personal resource endangered by her relatives' sense that it is or should already be theirs.

Although she thinks of herself as well off, her savings are, in fact, relatively modest. She lives in subsidized housing on a pension and savings.

Thus, the unpaid "borrowings" of her relatives represent a significant depletion of her finite reserves. She is torn between desiring to assist loved ones financially and personally and a sense of her own impending need. There is nobody to care for her as she cared for her mother, after all. And so the savings accrued over a lifetime will have to pay for whatever help she requires. And yet, she both wants and needs to be of assistance to her relatives. Thus, she finally accepts that what has been taken will not be returned while guarding against future raids on her savings, saying, "Never, never lend them your Visa card."

At this writing Sherry Busch is seventy-eight years old. She is slighter, frailer, and still indomitable. She has voluntarily given up her automobile license because of her physical limits, yet she remains extremely active. Others give her rides or she takes public transit. Although she has had to curtail her yoga classes, she continues to teach meditation at senior citizen homes in the city. And the days are still too short to contain her interests. Last week, lunch at her apartment was constantly interrupted by telephone calls from other seniors needing advice, friends "checking in," and administrators involved in programs she was committed to assisting. I asked if the money borrowed on her credit card seven years ago had ever been repaid. She laughed. "Bless them, no," she laughed. "I'll never see it this side of heaven."

NOTE

1. For a discussion of the use of money as a metaphor for a range of intergenerational tensions in elder care, see Tom Koch, *Mirrored Lives: Aging Children and Elderly Parents* (Westport, CT: Praeger, 1990).

2

Puck, and Damn Proud of It

To be seventy years young is sometimes far more cheerful than to be forty years old.
    Oliver Wendell Holmes, Sr. (letter to Julia Wood Howe, May 27, 1889)

Pasted on the wall of Jake Epp's living room, in Honolulu, Hawaii, above the table where he spent his days, was a bumper sticker that read: "Retired Army and Damn Proud of It." His military tenure was perhaps the most important element in his personal history, one that defined his life. Because of visual impairments, he could no longer read the words on the sticker when this interview was recorded in late 1989. By then he was a pensioner, half of whose $17,000 income went to paying his monthly rent. At the time of this interview he was seventy-five years old and a veteran of World War II, Korea, and Vietnam.

I worked in Honolulu for several years, and for much of that time we were neighbors. Over the years we became friends. Mr. Epp and I first met when he was still able to drive his car. In those days we were simply acquaintances, people who would nod to each other in passing as we entered or left the apartment building we shared. Later, when mobility and vision problems limited the range of his physical world, I would drop by his apartment several times a week. Sometimes I ran errands for him, although he liked to think of himself as self-sufficient.

He seemed pleased when I asked if I might tape a conversation, although he modestly insisted that "My stories aren't the type folks put into books."

But the idea of being in a book was exhilarating to him, I think—an affirmation. The first interview recorded for this project, it remains one of my favorites.

Once I ran, then I walked, and now I can barely crawl to the store. Instead of just striking out and moving around, I go step by step these days. I'm not going out as I wish and coming back the way that I want to. I hate to start out to the bus stop and then have to stop twice before I get there because my legs are so weak and tired. This is why I don't get out and around much anymore.

At one time, I had no hesitation about going to the market on foot. It was nice exercise and I enjoyed it. I could scamper on down to the Village Market a few blocks away down Wilder Street, especially on Sunday morning, pick up what I needed, stop in at the bakery, get a Sunday newspaper, and walk all the way back up to the apartment. Even though I had the car, I preferred to walk. Then, as time went by, it became a little more difficult. I would have to stop a couple times on the way to the market and lean up against a post or a fence and rest just a little bit. The same coming back home.

Then I discovered they had this little market around the corner from here, the one down on Pensacola Street in that condominium complex around the corner. If you don't know it's there, you'd never find it. It's on the corner of Pensacola and Davenport. I began to use that because it was a shorter trip for walking. Later on, the walking part was too hard for me to try and tackle anymore.

To go to the little store down on Pensacola, I normally have to stop about three times before I get to the market. It's my balance for one thing and my legs for the other, 'cause they aren't getting any stronger. I've been using lotion on my legs, and they seem to be feeling just a little bit better, but not too much stronger. My eyes are no better. The right one is the one that I think is affecting my balance, not the left one. The left one seems to be in good order. When I close my left eye, all I see of you is a blur, not a clear image.

I've been wearing these glasses now for several years, but they need to be corrected. You know, I can see better with my photo gray sunglasses than with the clear lenses. Even at night when I'm sitting here watching television, my sunglass lenses give me a clearer image than straight eyeglasses. I know it's no use getting behind the wheel of an automobile with my eyesight the way it is. No! That's why, when I discovered a buyer, I sold my Plymouth. That was a good automobile—my Green Hornet. What I do now is I pick up the telephone over there and I dial 944–5513. That's Royal Taxi

Company. Then I go down the steps and get right in the cab. It only takes 'em a few minutes to get here.

I read everything I could get my hands on from the time I was first able to read as a youngster up until just a few months ago. Now, well, I can remember, can't I? But I am still a great fan of Mr. Shakespeare. I have read, I think, every word Mr. Shakespeare ever wrote. I am especially fond of his play *The Merchant of Venice* in which the lady lawyer, Portia by name, says to Shylock, that money-lender: "You can have your pound of flesh but not an ounce of blood." [*Laughs.*] That was a lady with spine. Yes, sir! When I was young I even played a part in a play by Mr. Shakespeare in school. It was a play I've always liked, *A Midsummer Night's Dream*. I was Puck.

You see all the magazines I get, but I have trouble reading them now. I can't read that fine print anymore. I'm just looking at a blur. That's why I dragged out this old flashlight, but it's useless. This thing spreads out so you don't get the distinct letters that you would like. I need a penlight to read and then I'm all right. One bright light in one spot so you can read A, B, C, D, E. That's what I planned to ask you about. If and when you get around to a store that has those small, pocket-sized penlights—that's what I need. I had one before, but the bulb burned out in it. If only I could get this eye business settled, it would be much easier.

How do I spend my days? Scurrying around the apartment. Cleaning up here, cleaning up there. Rinsing out some soiled undershirts and shorts. Every day is a little piece of laundry being done. Polish some shoes. Bag up some trash. There are little things that can be done. This weekend there will be football between, I think, Hawaii and Colorado State. So I want to take that in. I'll watch the TV, as much as I'm able at least.

My friend Lonnie does all my accounting for me. And bill paying. And shopping. All I do is sign the checks. She's no relation whatsoever. How did I meet Lonnie? I was in a lounge one afternoon—this was when I was still driving. It was called Rocky's Lounge. They had a pair of boxing gloves up over the door. I knew Rocky, Rocky Salina, she was running the lounge. She had bought out my ex-wife who owned it before. So I was in Rocky's one afternoon, and I walked up to the bar and ordered a beer. I noticed this little mouse of a woman crouched over in the corner, in a booth. She was sitting over there not doing anything. There were almost no customers in the joint. Two or three. Anyway, I just got off the bar stool and went over and sat down in the chair across from her in the booth. And I asked her if she would like to have a drink. No, she didn't drink, she said. She doesn't drink today. And she doesn't smoke. Well, anyway, she got up out of the booth and went off somewhere.

I asked Rocky when she came into the lounge, "Who is that little girl who doesn't want to talk to anybody?" And she said, "Oh, that's Lonnie." I said, "Lonnie? Hawaiian?" And she said, "No, she's Vietnamese." The word Lon-ie in Vietnam means a flower, some kind of a flower.

Anyway, Lonnie and I became pretty good friends. I found out that she had a Honda Accord. She used to live down here on Haiouli Street and, I tell you, that girl had a scrumptious apartment. She lived up on the seventh floor. She invited me to her apartment one time, and I've never seen anything more immaculate than that apartment she had.

She comes maybe twice a week. Maybe I shouldn't tell you this. She writes all my checks. I just sign them. She brings my supplies. I write out a list of what I need and she brings it. That's how I get by, with Lonnie's help.

Children? Yes, I've got my daughter and her daughter. They live in a small town called Danning, Georgia. My son and his family, they live a little further north in Columbine. They've been there for quite a number of years. My son and his son and my son's wife, they never come to Hawaii. They never go anywhere except Columbine, Georgia. Of course, they go down to visit my daughter in Danning, but they never make any trips abroad.

I don't want to be one of those Georgia crackers. What would I do living out there in the country? My daughter's working. Her daughter's going to school. Her husband is working. So why would I want to go to Danning, Georgia, and do nothing when I'd rather do nothing right here? I like the neighborhood in which I'm living. And the independence. That's the greatest thing. I do not want to go back and impose myself on anyone.

You see, my wife had a mental disturbance. I had to have her hospitalized. And there I was, taking care of her and the kids. But I had to go back to Korea to make a living. So I put the kids in a foster home. That was what I had to do. In the army when they say go, you go. I wrote the institution and the foster home every week. They always said everything was fine—as long as I sent the money. Every week. But then my wife's family, and I don't know how, got her out. They signed some papers and got her released from the institution. I wrote and tried to find out where she was, but nobody every told me. So I really respect my son and daughter. They really had to raise themselves.

My daughter and her daughter came last year for ten days. They stayed right here and I slept there on the sofa. But when they were here, all they wanted to do was go to the beach. Every day. I showed them where the bus stop was, and they just went down there every day. Still, it was a fine visit.

After my first marriage, the one to my children's mother, I was married to one of those sweet, simple Korean women. I got her set up in this apartment. I remained working in Korea, she was over here. When the job assignment was over, I came home and she came too. I really thought that I was going to have a wonderful, long retirement. She didn't want me to go out and go back to work. She liked it fine. I sat around this apartment for about a month and didn't do anything but enjoy Christmas and New Year's. She got herself a job.

I could not see my wife supporting me when I had two good arms and two good legs. So I went job hunting. When I picked up a job as a condo manager, she didn't like that. I could tell. Yet she was working, managing a damn bar over on Young Street. She also managed one down in Kakaako area and another one up there on Kapiolani Boulevard. But I didn't complain to her about what her job was. She had her own hours and, of course, I had mine. I'd be at the bus stop down there across the street every morning by seven o'clock. My duty time started at eight. I was on the job site around 7:35 every morning, except Sunday.

Well, my Korean wife had become Americanized to the point where she didn't think that life together was the answer anymore. So she filed for divorce and moved out. I stayed here in the apartment. She still has relatives here in Honolulu, but I never see them. She has three nieces who at one time used to live here with her. One of them is now attending college in, ah, Los Angeles—that's the oldest one. The other two have graduated from McKinley High School here in Honolulu. So all three of those girls have turned out to be remarkably well educated. I can remember when the only English they knew was "Hi-Bye." That was it.

One of them is a very good-looking woman. They used to come here to visit pretty often. When they knew that I got off work at one o'clock on Saturday, they would come over and help cook dinner. We'd play the radio, the television. They were just like my own daughters. But once those three girls left the area, well, I don't know what they're doing now except the oldest one. She's the smartest character I think I've ever seen. She got nothing but straight As when she was going to school here in Honolulu and graduated with honors. I went to her graduation ceremony at McKinley High School. There's just nothing in this world like a smart girl.

Even after she left, my wife was calling on me, from time to time, for financial assistance. "Can you let me have $200? Can you let me have $400?"

I wondered why. She was just overspending more than she was making and was running into debt, even though she was driving around in a big Lincoln Continental. Did I give her the money? Foolishly, yes. I went to the bank and borrowed $1,500. I walked into her establishment and I laid it on the table and I said, "There you are." She was refurbishing the interior of the lounge and she needed the $1,500 to pay for new bar stools and various other things to dress it up. New chandelier lights.

The last time I saw that woman was over at Nuuanu Cemetery, where they have that little chapel. Her dad had passed away—Mr. Kim, who was a pretty nice Korean gentleman—and I was invited by her older sister. I had seen the notice in the obituary column. And that was the last time I saw my Korean wife, or ex-wife. Let's put it that way.

That job I picked up, at the condo? Even in my dreams, I'm on the job at Nuuanu Street. I was the building manager for this condominium, seventy-two units and twenty-seven floors. Now today is Friday. What would I be doing over at Nuuanu today? I would be running a vacuum cleaner over twenty-seven lobby carpets. Sure, I miss it. I did it so long and so often. I cleaned the pool. That was my Saturday specialty. And every Saturday morning, I was also checking the trash chute that came all the way down into a trash room and into these steel holders on wheels.

I started to work over there in February 1976 and I worked that job exactly five years to the day. It wasn't, you know, high-paying job, but at least it was an income. I have seen about all the sights there are to see on this island. And not just on this island, Oahu. But also in Korea, Japan, Vietnam, and Thailand for a short period of time. I was also in Germany and France and England. All for the army. Everything that I have ever done since I was in a working status has been for the U.S. Army. The whole bit. I was a fire marshal when I was in Europe. That's when I was wearing the [lieutenant's] bars. But mainly what I think about, now, is the work that I have done here in Honolulu. It just keeps coming back to me.

I learned so much on the job, that was the greatest part of it. I met everybody in the whole building, practically. There was a storage room down by my office. Well, I called it an office, but it was actually a shop next to the pump and hot water room. People always knew where to find me on Saturday. "Oh Mr. Epp, can I get into the storage room?" "Yes, ma'am." Unlock the storage room, let the lady go in. Everyone had an area in the storage room. Or some guy would come down and want to know if I would unlock the gate in case somebody came to call.

Having only one individual trying to accommodate everybody in that building was sometimes a hassle. I knew what my job was supposed to be, but these other little things creep into your job schedule. So why make out a schedule? And I never did, the whole five years that I was there.

It comes back to me. Yep, many facets of it, because I found out so much about the building that nobody had ever told me. I just had to learn it on my own. I had water schematics, true. I had electrical schematics, true. But the other parts of the building that you don't see in a drawing, those I had to figure out for myself. Like where all the valves were that you use to drain out the waste water system. I didn't know where they were. I didn't have any map or schematic to show me. I just went around the building and figured it out.

After I retired from the job in Nuuanu, I was sitting here doing nothing. I'd been out to Tripler Army Hospital here—I can go as a veteran, of course—for a little work on my teeth. One day, I get a telephone call from my old boss. He says, "Hey, I've got a part-time job for you, if you'd like to have it." So I want to know what he's talking about. He said, "We had to fire a fella from the job," and he said they needed somebody to take his place. It was three hours a day, five days a week. So that means fifteen hours a week at $5.50 an hour.

Well, I wasn't doing anything, why not take a chance? It was over on Lusitana Street, building number 1231. It was a condo, but a small one, only forty units. Yard work was the most important part—cleaning up the leaves, mowing the lawn. And, of course, cleaning down the stairwell. It was a three-floor building. I did that for two years. It was work. And now I can't, not anymore.

When I was wounded in France, the sciatic nerve in my left thigh was damaged. And as far as I know, even today, I'm still struggling around with some tiny pieces of shrapnel in my thigh. I took a hell of a big hit one night. The doctors thought they would have to amputate, but they managed to get by without it. The damn shrapnel went in and then it went up. Even in Korea, years later I got a piece out. It had worked its way from the inside of the thigh to the outside. I was getting an itchy sensation, and then I picked out a little piece of steel from under my skin. So anytime I have an operation that affects the left portion of my body, it means that sciatica is going to come back and haunt me. And it does. It certainly does.

If only this eye thing could be straightened out. But I won't go to Tripler [*Army Hospital*] again. No, sir. I'm finished with them. It takes six months to get an appointment there, maybe a year. Then I have to take a cab out there and wait all day. They looked at me and said there was no disease in my eyes and gave me some new glasses. But they don't do any good. Maybe it's the glasses, but I don't think so. I've seen these LensCrafters store ads on TV. That's where I'm going to go. If I have to pay $100 to do so, I'll just put it on my card. I have a MasterCard. That's what it's for.

I plan to live to be a hundred. I am surely working on that. But if I can't live the way I want, with my beer and cigarettes, well sir, I'd rather die tomorrow. All the time I was working I never drank on the job. Not in the army, not at Nuuanu or on Lusitania Street. I always liked my beer after work though, I did. And I always said that, someday, I'd be retired and would have a beer whenever I wanted. And that's what I do. Nobody to say different. And if I can't live like I wish, well, I'd as soon finish it all today. I would. I don't want anybody to ever put me in a place where they won't let me have my beer when I want or a smoke. No sir.

I never try and look at anything from the dim side. There was a song we used to sing, "What's the use of worrying, it never was worth while. So smile, smile, smile!" That's me. And I enjoy sitting still for a while. This jumping around in the army just didn't show me anything. Of course, in the army—as in any military service—a person is subject to discipline and orders. And I learned very quickly, when I got in the army, to do as I was told. If they said, "Pack your bags, you're going to Japan." Or you're going to Korea or you're going here or you're going there—I did so. And I knew, just as soon as I hung the window curtains, I'd be getting orders to move again. And now, no one tells me when I have to shave. No one tells me when I have to comb my hair. Now finally I can do as I want.

POSTSCRIPT

In recent years researchers have recognized that patient lives may be severely limited by cataracts even when a cursory examination shows, as it apparently did in this case, minimal clouding.[1] Physicians are therefore now urged to rely on a patient's subjective statements rather than simply on the results of a visual examination. Mr. Epp is a case in point. At the time of this interview he was functionally blind. With or without the aid of a flashlight he could barely read letters or telephone numbers written by me at his request, even when they were printed in block letters an inch in height. His sensitivity to light and the use of a flashlight for focusing on written materials most probably resulted from undiagnosed and untreated cataracts, or less likely some other problem.

For the better part of a year I urged him to make an appointment at Tripler Hospital for a new eye examination. As a veteran, it was his health insurer and provider. His assertion that it might take a calendar year to get an appointment—and years longer if he required real treatment—was, to me, frankly unbelievable. But at a gerontology conference in Honolulu I described Mr. Epp's symptoms to a Tripler physician and asked how long it would take to get an appointment for a man whose eyesight was so manifestly limited. He told me it might take a year for him to be seen by an optometrist and a second year before an ophthalmologist could be consulted. Surgery would require a third year's wait. If the mobility problems were related to neurologic and not visually based, well, that would require more waiting for appointments with various specialists before a diagnosis could be made. Mr. Epp died several months after that conference, still waiting for an appointment.

Jake Epp was a fairly typical "social drinker" who became an alcoholic after vision and mobility problems reduced his range from the city at large to the neighborhood and from there to the confines of our apartment building. Unable to read or to perceive images on a TV, beer and cigarettes became his constant companions. There were also occasional visits by Lonnie and me, of course, and, rarely, from one or another former acquaintance. Typically they were more common in the early days of his disability—when his absence from this bar or that club was noticed—than in the years spent alone and in his apartment.

He drank, by his own account, between ten and twelve beers a day. I took out his garbage most weeks and was fairly certain the count was closer to fifteen beers. Whenever I visited—whether at nine o'clock in the morning or ten o'clock at night, he had a newly opened beer by his side. My impression was that he would drink from the time he woke up until an early afternoon nap, and then drink again until dinner. In the early evening he would have a second nap, dozing, and then drink some more into the early hours of the day.

A social worker would have been horrified by Mr. Epp's lifestyle. Every night he prepared dinner from the food Lonnie had brought; sometimes a can of chili or hash, sometimes a frozen prepared meal. Breakfast and lunch were usually alcoholic meals, however, sometimes chased with peanuts or toast or salty potato chips. Although his apartment was fairly clean—its sweeping was an important part of his daily routine—his bathroom was a disaster—impossibly filthy and indescribably rank. And although he did his laundry every day, his pants legs were often stained with urine or excrement, a result of balance and vision problems as much as alcoholism, I believed.

Several times I considered calling social services and asking them to send a social worker to "assess" his needs. My suspicion was that he would be declared incompetent and then forcibly moved into a long-term care home. That, however, was his fear. He was adamant that he preferred his life as it was to anything so regimented as a group home. He had, he said, spent too many years in the military to look forward to barracks-style, close companionship again. He would not have thanked me for my intervention, and I decided that my sensibilities should not be used to deprive him of the life he chose.

I remained uncertain as to how to assist this man whom I liked in all his complexity. He was at once the career army fireman and lieutenant, a country boy who worked his way up and out into and around the world, and a bon vivant who talked familiarly about the bars and women he had known from Laos to Georgia. And yet, this self-educated reader who laughed familiarly at Portia's "spine" was also a functionally blind alcoholic unaware of his bodily functions. I could never decide which he needed more: social assistance or to be left alone. As a result, I did nothing but suffer occasional pains of liberal guilt while visiting his apartment several times a week.

My assumption was that sooner rather than later he would fall and injure himself. Then the ambulance would come, and, once hospitalized, folks with more certainty than I would decide he was unable to live alone. He then would be remanded to a veterans center where beer would be prohibited and cigarettes sparingly rationed.

Mr. Epp fooled us all. He died quietly one night , a beer beside him and a spent cigarette stub in his right hand. A heart attack, they said. After his death his son finally visited to collect his remains and a few personal odds and ends from Mr. Epp's apartment. Everyone told me how sad it was that he had died that way. "Yes, of course," I said. "A pity." Privately, however, I was relieved for myself—no more dilemma—and proud of Jake Epp. It was an ending he had anticipated, I think, if not one consciously chosen. He had said he would rather die than surrender his life to a nursing home where he would live among strangers while being bossed by women he did not know. Instead, he died at home and with his memories. With him at the end were the cigarettes and beer that I considered a foolish addiction but, to him, were symbols of independence.

NOTE

1. Eric B. Bass, Stacy Willis, and Ingrid U. Scott, Preference Values in Visual States in Patients Planning to Undergo Cataract Surgery, *Medical Decision Making* 17 (1997): 324–330.

3

A Russian Spring

Youth is a blunder;
Manhood a struggle;
Old Age a regret.

Benjamin Disraeli, 1844

Born into a Russian family that fled the Soviet Union after the Bolshevik Revolution, Alex Sarnoff grew up first in Europe and later in the United States as a member of a close-knit Russian emigrant community. As an adult, his working years were spent in Washington, D.C., as a government translator (he read or spoke Russian, German, English, and passable French). His son, Jon, is a journalist and sometime foreign correspondent; his daughter, Marie, lives in Berlin, where her husband works as a foreign correspondent.

I had known Mr. Sarnoff since his son and I first worked together in the early 1970s. I interviewed him while he visited Jon and his family who lived for a time in Honolulu, Hawaii, while I, too, was working there. The interview occurred the day before Mr. Sarnoff's visit ended; he was excited about traveling to visit his sister-in-law in California on her seventy-sixth birthday. Thus, the talk began with memories of her caregiving and the eventual institutionalization of her husband.

It was very difficult for my sister-in-law. My brother was almost an invalid. He couldn't walk. He was not in a wheelchair, but he was living at home and mostly sitting in an easy chair, watching TV. She had to help him whenever he had to go to the bathroom or get in and out of bed. I don't know exactly how it started. Maybe in the beginning he was capable of walking, but finally she had to get him admitted to a nursing home. He objected. He didn't want to go. He wanted to stay home and be taken care of. But finally she just couldn't manage, couldn't take it anymore. She had to call the fire department one day because he fell and she was unable to get him up.

It was a big burden on her, but she did it. She never complained. She was a remarkable wife. It probably was selfish of him not to want to go to a nursing home. All I can tell you is what I know from his wife, and she never complained. But she told me she had a very hard time, a very hard time taking care of him for the two or three years before he died. Well, he finally agreed to move to a nursing home and he stayed there for the final five or six months until he died. And we all knew that because she was in touch with my wife and with her parents in New York.

I remember him when he was younger and quite active. He was always a determined person. He was also, as far as I can remember, a despot. His wife was his obedient servant. He was very strong-willed. Maybe not strong, but he wanted to have his own way. Oh, this was about forty years ago when they were both much younger, when they had children—they had two children, a girl and a boy. I remember that she went through a very difficult period of adjustment. She was even contemplating divorce. But they never did. They didn't split because of the children. She also felt that it was her duty to take care of him.

She worked. They both worked. They both had jobs. I remember him when he was in his forties, because it was after they moved to California. They had been living in New York and he was working for Macy's department store. He was very proud, very happy to be the head of the glove department at Macy's. He always bragged about it. He was really trying to be a successful businessman. But he didn't get along very well with his in-laws, you see. My sister-in-law's parents lived in New York, her mother and father. And her mother and father didn't get along very well with him either.

Then they moved to California in the late forties or early fifties. He wanted to take his wife away from her family. And she followed him because she was an obedient wife, a beautiful wife. And they've been living in California ever since. In California, he became a real-estate salesman. He was buying and selling houses, but he was always a big spender. He wanted the best. He was a little bit of a showman. Anyway, that is my sister who I am going to visit in California.

As for me, after my wife's death, I left our house where we had lived together in Washington on June 1, 1978, and went to Staten Island. I retired in April 1978. I took early retirement. I moved to Staten Island into an old-age home called St. Damien the Cross. It was a retirement home for people of Slavic descent—Russians, Ukrainians, Poles. But there were a lot of other Americans there: Italians, Spanish. My son, Jon, told me this was a good thing, to get away from the old house. Memories. I didn't have a job anymore and needed a complete change of scenery. So we rented the old house for revenue.

But I was very unhappy there at St. Damien. I only stayed two months. I was sixty-two years old, but most of the people there were in their seventies or eighties or even nineties. It was an old-age home! I had a nice room. It was a four-story building, a former Marriott Hotel or a Ramada Inn or something, I'm not sure. They had two hundred people there, men and women.

It was not a nursing home. I mean, most of these people were able to walk. They were not invalids. We had to come down for breakfast. They gave us breakfast, lunch, and dinner. The food was horrible. The first person I met there was an old lady I'd known before. She was in her eighties. I knew her very well—she was also Russian and the mother of a good friend of mine. She used to live with her son and daughter-in-law in their house in Washington. Probably they didn't want to take care of her because she had a nasty character, although she was quite healthy. So they put her in that old-age home, where she was very unhappy. She was always complaining. When I arrived she asked me, "What are you doing here? Why are you here? You don't belong here." And she started complaining about the food, the people. It was a very unpleasant experience.

I tried at first to sort of adapt myself. I was able to walk. I didn't have a cane in those days. We played shuffleboard. There was a sort of parking lot. Have you been to Staten Island? I had never lived on Staten Island before. I don't have very pleasant memories of that.

Jon was the one who helped me move there. We were in touch. He came to visit me with another friend of his, John Coleman, and they were very nice, took me for a ride.

Jon even brought me my car. He lived in Baltimore then. And when I first got to Staten Island, I had no car. I had to take a bus. They had restaurants and such around, and I was trying to get away from the place as much as possible. Jon said to me, "You want your car? Okay, I'll bring your car." So he brought me my old Chevy Impala. In those days I had a 1972 Chevrolet Impala—a nice big car.

Jon took me to the beach. You know, Jon always likes to explore places. He showed me the ferry from Staten Island to Manhattan, downtown. But I was feeling very lonely. I couldn't make friends with all these old people, you know. I was assigned a table in the dining room with an old lady and so I had all my meals with her. She was constantly complaining. I just couldn't get along very well.

So I told Jon I was not very happy and he told me, "Come on. If you're not happy here, let's go back to Washington. We'll try to find an apartment for you." So we went back to Washington. I drove my old Chevrolet and he drove his car all the way from Staten Island to Washington. We drove to-gether. And he found an apartment for me on Connecticut Avenue just across from the zoo. It was an apartment house. I moved there in August 1978. In the end I stayed only two months, from June to August, on Staten Island.

When I got back to Washington I had this apartment, furnished. I had a bed, a table, a chair. Very spare, I mean, but it was a nice apartment. Well, I got very depressed then, because all the people I knew in Washington had left. Many people leave the city in the hottest part of the summer, you know. Anyway, those who can get out, do. It was the middle of summer and it was hot! Jon was working in Baltimore then, so I was on my own. I drove around. I went to the zoo many times. The zoo was my main occupation, just across the street.

Then I called up some people I knew and told them I was back in Wash-ington. One day I got a telephone call from a woman who said, "I heard you're living here in Washington, alone. You know, I'd like to ask you to do me a favor. My mother is living alone, in Arlington, Virginia. She has a house. My father, her husband, just died, he died in June." I didn't really re-member her when she called me, but I knew who she was. And she told me, "Would you like to move in? Would you like to stay with my mother for two weeks? I'm going on a vacation, and she doesn't want to be living alone, es-pecially at night."

She was Russian. I lived at her house from 1978 to 1986, when I moved to Florida. She was a remarkable woman. I hadn't known her very well. I'd met her socially, so we just had to get acquainted, you see. And we got along very well. She gave me a room downstairs. She had a very small house, two bedrooms. Her bedroom was upstairs. She had to walk up a very steep flight of steps, and the room she offered to me was downstairs. The first two weeks I spent there I was just a guest.

We got along very well. One day she said, "If you want to move in, I'd be very happy." And she told me how much I'd have to pay. I paid rent, of course. That's how it was. So I moved out of my apartment in Washington. Jon again helped me move to Arlington, which is just across the river, you know—a suburb of Washington. And I moved into her house as a border, which included room and board. She was very active, this woman. Very energetic. She was a very good cook, too. Yes, she was. She made some delicious dinners and I felt at home. This was the first time since my wife died in 1975 that I was living with another person.

No, I have to correct myself. Actually, after my wife died in 1975 I had roomers at the old house. Room and board for $100 a month, one room. I had three people. The first person I had was John Capellino. He was a divorced man in his forties who was living in Maryland and wanted to share a house. We got along very well, but he stayed only one year. He eventually moved to New York. The second person who moved in was Harvey Weissman and he was really quite a character. He came over to my house and told me he was in Washington living with his sister on Massachusetts Avenue. He said, "My sister is very well off. She has a condominium. She has a beautiful place, but we don't get along. I'd like to move out." He asked me if he could move in and I said, "Sure, go ahead." He was a fanatical anti-smoker. He had been smoking heavily and had only one lung left. And whenever I lit my pipe, he became furious. He would tell me, "You're killing yourself. You're going to end up with lung cancer. You have only a couple more years to live." He became very obnoxious, you know. And maybe I became a little bit too familiar with him. But I wanted company. I enjoyed having someone in the house.

He finally moved out. We had been talking about Sara, my daughter who has mental problems, and he started telling me that it was probably all my fault, that I'd been a bad father. I started to share things, to talk about my problems, and he became very involved, very critical. I finally told him, "Harvey, I think I have another man interested in the house." My third boarder was a young student who was studying at Georgetown University and wanted to learn Russian.

Later, living in the house in Arlington I felt that I was—maybe I should say quite frankly—it was the first time in a long time that I had someone to take care of me [*laughs*]. Before that, I had to take care of myself. After my wife died, I'd been on my own. I think my landlady in Arlington was a sort of mother-figure to me. She was twenty years older than me. She had a big heart. She was a remarkable woman but she was by no means a clever woman. Sometimes she would say some very stupid things, but she was very, very kind. She was an exceedingly kind person, and I felt at ease with her.

We got along very well. Those were happy years, from 1978 until 1983. We went out a lot. I had a car, she had a car. She went shopping on her own sometimes, but she was a very poor driver. Her daughter always got mad at her: "Why do you drive? You're taking a chance with your life. Once you drove into a one-way street the wrong way!" She was an old lady! She was in her eighties already. We went walking together. She was in very good health. She was getting a little bit hard of hearing, gradually. She was a cozy person to live with, you know. We were very close and we had a lot of friends in common. We went to visit some friends that I knew, that she knew. Older friends, all people of our age, seniors. We went to church together. For the first time I felt that I had, not a family, but a companion. Exactly. That's the word.

All this came to an abrupt halt when we had an automobile accident in 1983. She was hurt. She had a broken hip and was in the hospital for two months. I wasn't hurt at all. We were on our way to visit her daughter who lived in Richmond. We used to go and visit her daughter once a week almost all year 'round. She was divorced and had two lovely girls. Then the accident. Bam! Like that, things changed.

After the accident my landlady had an operation, and I was again on my own. I went to visit her, of course. My car was towed away—it was considered a total loss. The whole front and right side were broken, the windshield was shattered. It happened so quickly, so unexpectedly. It happened at an intersection of two big streets in Arlington. We were driving at night around eight o'clock. The weather was awful. It was rainy and cold, and we collided with another car that was trying to make a left turn. The woman failed to yield the right of way when I was in the middle of the intersection and had the green light. She plowed into my car.

My landlady didn't come home from the hospital for at least two months. Her daughter was visiting every day, and I visited almost every day as well. Then, in February 1984, I came to visit Jon who was working here in Hawaii. That was the first time he worked here, I think. I needed a little breather, you know. After she got out of the hospital, she was transferred to a nursing home. She had physical therapy there. She had to learn to walk with a walker. Mind you, she was already in her eighties when it happened.

I stayed with Jon in Hawaii for ten days or so. When I went back in the middle of February, my landlady was already home. She had a nurse who was taking care of her because she was an invalid now. I moved upstairs. My room before the accident was downstairs, but my landlady's daughter told me, "When Mother comes home, you'll have to move upstairs. She can't walk up that flight of steps anymore." It was a converted attic where my landlady slept before the accident. In fact, I moved upstairs before I went to Hawaii.

We just continued living in the same house. I didn't think of moving out at the time. Then things got a bit nasty because of this woman who was taking care of my friend. She was surprised I was there. My landlady and I, we were quite attached to each other. Then this accident. Then this nurse who was a stranger to her and to me. The nurse was cooking, she was running the house. She was in charge! And I felt like an outsider. My dear old landlady kept telling me, "Don't pay attention when she gets mad at you. When she gets nasty. Don't pay attention. I want you to stay here." She didn't want me to leave, you know. She didn't want me to leave at all, but I was beginning to get a little bit frustrated.

Now Jon was again instrumental in my moving. He kept telling me, "Why are you staying with this old lady? She's not your mother, she's your landlady. She's not a relative. You're not obliged to stay here. If you're not happy, why don't you move out?" Jon is the one who actually talked me into then moving to Florida. Before I went to Florida in 1985, a close friend of mine died. Mariette was also an old lady I'd known for many years. We would visit often, even after the accident. She lived on Quebec Street right off Connecticut Avenue. She had lost her husband in 1975, the same year my wife died. She was a very good friend of mine and also of my landlady's. They knew each other. They were both about the same age. Her name was Mariette Bedrusian. She died in February. The night before she died, she complained she wasn't feeling well. And she had always been in very good health. She was a strong woman, and she died of a heart attack in the night. This was also a big shock to me and to my landlady. We lost a very good friend.

After Mariette's death, Jon arranged a cruise for me. So I went down to Miami and took a cruise. Jon was very helpful. He is a good son, you know. He told me, "You have to get away from it all." I went on a four-day cruise to the Bahamas. It was very nice, a real getaway. I liked it, but I had to come back again. Finally, I moved to Florida in May 1986.

I must say frankly I was very attached to my landlady. We were very close. I was, well, Jon probably couldn't understand because he told me all the time, "She's not your mother. Come on, you're free. You're young enough to live somewhere else." But I had a very hard time making up my mind what was the right thing to do because my landlady wanted me to stay. And her daughter was very happy that I was staying there. Actually, I was of no help because she had this nurse who was taking care of her. I was her friend. That was the only thing that kept me there for such a long time.

Finally my son said, "Come on." He gave me a push. We went down to Florida again to look around in January 1986. I told my landlady, "I'm going down to Florida with my son." She began to sense that something was cooking. Later she told me, "Your children, especially Jon, want you to leave me. They are the ones who are trying to talk you into leaving me, moving out." She was upset about that. And I realized I was making her unhappy. It bothered me. I realized that I was being selfish. We had been living together peacefully and very well.

When I went down to Florida, I didn't tell her that I was going to move there. I told her we were going for a week. We had made arrangements, we had called people, and we stayed in Florida for a week—in Gulf Port, where I live now. So when we came back, I had to tell her. I feel maybe I shouldn't have told her right away. I should have been more tactful. But she asked me point-blank, "How do you like Florida? Do you want to move to Florida?" And I said, "Well, yes." She froze, and then she got very mad. She said, "Then I don't want you to stay here any longer. You have a son in Baltimore. I want you to go and live with him tomorrow."

I was not only surprised, I was also disturbed. She became hostile. Although she was a very kind person, she sometimes had crazy moods and would say things like, "I don't want you anymore. I want you to leave." I didn't move right away. I stayed with my landlady from January until May. And those last three months—February, March, April—were very unpleasant.

When I moved in May 1986, Jon helped again. First I rented a room again, like I did in Arlington, in a private home where a Russian lady was living. We were getting along very well, but then something happened. About two weeks after I moved in, suddenly a man came by. He walked right into the house—a perfect stranger—and he told me, pointing at my landlady, Mrs. Karpov, "She's my fiancée. We're getting married." Now this woman never told me she had a boyfriend or a man who wanted to marry her. And then I began to think about getting out. A couple days later, we were sitting on the porch and the man told me in Russian, "You are disturbing us."

So then I began looking around and, thank God—God helped me a lot, I must say—I found my present apartment. I met my present landlady by chance. A chance meeting. She told me she had an apartment for rent and would be willing to take me. I went over to look at her apartment and right away I said, "Yes, I'm moving in." So in June of that year I moved into my present apartment.

I am again on my own. I have my own kitchen, my own bathroom. I cook, but I'm not a very good cook. To be frank, I'm a very poor cook. I open cans, I buy cold cuts, soup. I eat a lot of soup. I was never able to cook very well. Maybe I'm too lazy. Maybe I should learn to cook, I don't know.

Now my legs are becoming a problem. They hurt and my balance has been bad since 1978, when I was still living in Arlington and went to see a neurologist. This neurologist told me, "You have a degeneration of the cerebellum, which causes poor balance."[1] He questioned me very closely: "Do you drink? How much do you drink, and what do you drink?" I told him I used to drink occasionally. I used to enjoy a gin and tonic in the summer, which I don't do anymore. When I lived with my landlady, we used to have wine with dinner, a white wine. We had cocktails. Now that I'm alone, I don't drink. I drink socially when invited, but I don't have liquor at home. I drink a lot of juices.

Would I like to live with my kids? Of course. But I know that's impossible. They don't want me. Why should they? I wouldn't mind living with my daughter, Marie. I know that Jon and his wife are very active, very busy, and they have a little girl. I would be in the way. And my daughter, who is now forty-five years old, she's busy with her life, too. Her children are all growing up, they're teenagers. We see each other in the summer when Marie goes to Quebec. They have a little cottage up there, on a lake. They bought that little cottage six or seven years ago and they love it. They go every year and spend two months. I visit, and sometimes Jon visits with his family, too. I'm very happy there. Maybe because I'm taken care of [*laughs*]. It's this business of being taken care of.

I don't think they'd want me very much. That is, there is no place for me to live in their lives. It's not that they don't love me. I understand that. In the old days, a hundred years ago, old people stayed at home. Usually, there were three generations living together. Grandma and Grandpa, Mama and Papa, and the children. Sometimes the grandchildren as well. Now old people have to live on their own, either like I do or in an old-age home, a nursing home. Old people are becoming more and more pushed aside. I don't think old people are quite capable of being independent. Some are. Maybe I'm wrong here. Maybe I want to be dependent. Maybe I'm fighting something.

I know the emphasis is on senior citizens. They're not even called old people anymore, they're called "seniors." "The best years of your life," people are told. "Life starts at sixty." For me, no. Definitely not. The best years were the early years of my marriage, which were also not very easy. After all, I was in the U.S. army from 1942 to 1945. Then, maybe, the second-best years were when I was in school, when I was about fourteen, fifteen, six-teen—a teenager. I loved my school. Good years!

Summing up, all in all I was quite unprepared. But that's life. You can't stop it and, really, there is no preparation for it. This is something every-body has to resign himself to. Jon, Marie, everyone's getting older. Some people grow older and older but they don't feel it. They're enjoying their senior years. I admire such people. My landlady in Arlington was such a person. She never felt old. She never talked about her age—until this stu-pid accident. If we hadn't had that accident, I'm sure she'd have been in good health with a cheerful disposition until her death. She died last year in January at the age of ninety-three.

POSTSCRIPT

I always called him Mr. Sarnoff, never Alex. Over the years of his travels we met perhaps fifteen times, either when he came to Hawaii to visit his son or when he lived in Washington, on my infrequent trips to that city.

It would be easy, too easy, to use him as an example of the dependent male, of a generation of men who needed women to care for and maintain them. He could not cook and he did not clean. Certainly, he lacked Mr. Epp's sense of self-reliance, the puckish spirit of cheerful independence that characterized that man's peripatetic life.

Alex Sarnoff sought in his later years what in his early life he had taken for granted. He was, after all, an immigrant raised in a community of Rus-sian emigrés whose language and culture were in America but not Ameri-can. In his later years he wanted friends of his age and culture, companions of a background and class who could support him in what, for Mr. Sarnoff, was an eternally foreign, impersonal world. And so he paid rent to live in the houses of women with whom he spoke a common language. He rented rooms less out of financial necessity than because of his desire for the scent of food and a pattern of culture that was an essential element in his life.

Jon Sarnoff periodically urged his father to enjoy his liberty and not be burdened by old associations, old alliances, old ties. "Why are you staying with this old lady?" he asked his father. "She's your landlady, not a relative. You're not obliged to stay here." That Mr. Sarnoff felt comfortable with his landladies, tied to them in ways that were fulfilling and not limiting, was something Jon did not understand and Mr. Sarnoff could not explain.

And yet, what Alex Sarnoff sought most was not comfort but the ap-proval of his children. And so, at their urging, he moved. Unable to live with his children, he tried instead to accept their advice, to live the life they expected him to enjoy. What he most wanted, however, they could not give: a home in their homes, a life of children and grandchildren that combined his culture and their world. "I don't think they'd want me very much," he said. "That is, there is no place for me to live in their lives." Their worlds were filled with busy careers and growing families. It is what he had hoped they would achieve. But their achievements came at the—to him—terrible price of a place in their daily lives. He was not, after all, a man to prepare the meals or do housework as a way of contributing to their households. As a baby-sitter for young children he was nervous and uncertain. And so he lived with Russian landladies, eagerly anticipating each visit only to feel estranged and useless once he was at a child's home. "I'm there and not there," he confided to me in one of our discussions. "I am at odds with it all, you know?"

"I was quite unprepared," Mr. Sarnoff said. He was right. Neither the world he came from nor the world he inhabited as a translator prepared him for a time of lonely independence and moderate disability. And so he spent these years seeking a life that would have the flavor of a culture he grew up in, a country he barely remembered. It was a quintessentially American tragedy.

Mr. Sarnoff's balance problems slowly worsened. Like Mr. Epp, he walked with increasing care. Unlike the latter, however, Alex Sarnoff never developed an American sense of bonhomie. He lived instead with an immigrant's sense of loss, of worlds lost. It is, some say, a Russian trait.

When Mr. Sarnoff died, his son, Jon, was in Hong Kong and his daughter, Marie, was in Berlin. He died still estranged from his other daughter, Sara, still regretting the automobile accident that injured the landlady who had been his friend. I learned of his dying from Jon, who in a letter said, "I know how much you liked him, and how much he liked you. You were his friend."

NOTE

1. This is a common result of alcoholism, which explains the neurologist's questions. As in this case, however, it is also symptomatic of a host of other neurologic problems.

4

A Nursing Life

The crux of it all, perhaps, the real secret, is that there was
nobody to rub the gentle oil into Mrs Tolbert's itch. She was
alone, and unprepared to be so.

M.F.K. Fisher, *Sister Age*

Holly Treeson is the stereotypical senior: a widowed, fragile, house-bound
woman dependent on social services for her maintenance. She is also a fine
example of the limits of that general stereotype. We met through my friend
and her physician, Dr. Bill McArthur. He thought she needed companionship, someone to take an interest in her. "You should meet her," he said to me
one day when I was visiting Vancouver, B.C. "You'll learn a lot." He arranged
a meeting for us in 1992, and then, at a second meeting in her apartment, we
recorded this interview. After that Holly and I became friends, talking on
the phone when I was away, visiting when I was in Vancouver.

Osteoporosis, congestive heart failure, clinical depression: What the
gross facts of her medical condition did not reveal was the intelligence of the
woman, her ability to perceive herself within a broader history, to see her life
within the trend lines of both medical and social changes. For that, one
needed to listen to her, to watch as she grappled between past experience
and future hopes for a place in the daily world.

Being alone—and I don't mean living alone but not having anyone to
discuss things with—is one thing that older people know. No one is
interested in what they want. You sort of lose your self-esteem and

your dignity. You don't have someone to go places with you, someone who would like to travel with you through the northern regions of the provinces, things like that. You just don't have any of those things anymore. This year I had four sisters-in-law and two very close friends die. Actually, they all died last spring. And that's left a big hole. You don't make new friends, particularly when you are, like me, pretty well immobile.

I can't go out by myself. My friends and I used to talk on the phone and that sort of thing. Most of them were right here in Vancouver. They took me out for drives and out for dinner, you know, things like that. And we went to classes at the college, and one of them would always be there. Particularly Mabel, she was an exceptional woman. She had been a teacher and then started Burnaby College for the retired, you know. Now that she's gone, there's a big hole in my life. She got me interested in things when my Mum was still here, too. Often Mum, who I cared for, built barriers so I couldn't go out, even if I could get a homemaker to come in. I think she wanted me to go places, but she also didn't want to be left alone.

Ten years I cared for her. The first four years she was mobile, she was very active. She had a sharp mind. But it was my home she was in and she couldn't recognize that. She couldn't see the inflation, that things cost more. She couldn't see why she should give me any of her money to keep things going. She wasn't going to help me with the mortgage.

She had eight children but I was the only one who was single, and also I was a nurse. And Mother used to say to me when I had to bathe her, "That's why I made you a nurse." [*Laughs*.] But did she want me to be a nurse when I went to school? Not particularly. She was a very hard sell as far as education. Still, we all managed. Three of my sisters are teachers, and one of my brothers is a brewmaster. Two of my brothers went to war, and one died on his twenty-first birthday. In fact, today would have been his birthday. My oldest brother was a Conservative Party organizer.

When I was four years old—I can remember it so well—I remember skipping around Mum's bed when she had heart problems. She worked very, very hard. She sort of impressed on me that I was to look after the family. You see, I was the oldest girl. We sisters were born close together. I looked after them when we were small and I think they resented that terribly. Mum wasn't well, and I was to look after the family. I think there was a lot of resentment on their side because, well, in those days you never talked about such things. I mean, it never occurred to me until I was fifty to think, "Where is *my* life?" By that time my husbands had died and my kids had gone. It's a hard job, to learn that, because your inclination is to look after others. I had ten years to myself.

My mother came to me when I was sixty. It was during those ten years be-fore that—when I was "independent," you know?—that I very foolishly married again and it was a dreadful mistake. It didn't last long, and it was part of my upset, too. But mother always said I didn't do a very good job looking after myself. [*Laughs.*] Just builds you up, you know?

My mother had a type of leukemia, and she had a lot of arthritis in her spine. She liked to walk, but she lost so much strength. She was treated for it with chemotherapy only when the blood count got particularly high, but then she got to where she was bedridden. After all those years of bedpans, urinals, and sponge baths, it was still hard the first time for me when I had to care for her. Yeah, I think so. It was very hard for my mother, too. She really felt indignant when I had to bathe her and put things on her, especially dia-pers and things like that. Most of the time she was quite lucid. She knew ex-actly what was going on. I had quite a bit of empathy for her, actually.

She was easy in lots of ways in terms of taking food and other such things, and for a while, you see, I could take her for doctor's appointments, take her out, and things like that. But then it got to be too much for her to go out, and finally I was having so much trouble with my back that I simply had to stop driving the car. But by then, my grandchildren were driving it more than I was. I had three sisters right in Vancouver and they would come with their families, but no way could I go out for a walk or do some-thing else while they were here. They were strictly there to visit Mum and to be fed. I was the caregiver, the nurse. And because Mum was very hospi-table she didn't let someone come and not offer food. But I had to buy, pre-pare, and serve it. Of course, I'm still angry about it. Even today, I don't want any of them in my house. Did I tell them how I felt? No, I didn't. I al-ways have to think about things. I'm not good right off.

Speaking of nursing, the care people got then was tremendous. It's get-ting so the personal care you get in the hospital these days is nil. Today you have to care for yourself, even when you're very ill. When I was in for my hip operation, well that was a dreadful experience. You never saw anybody except to have a needle stuck into you. There was absolutely no personal care. And in my day I really liked bedside nursing. When I worked in nurs-ing homes I couldn't bear to see a person alone when they're suffering or dy-ing. If it's past my time on shift, all right. I still have to stay there. They need that comfort. To leave someone when they're really suffering, I just couldn't do it. That was the job.

In the early days, my training was my first time away from home. I started in January 1938 at St. Paul's Hospital here in Vancouver.[1] I worked at home four years before I went into training. I got out of school when I was so young—I was maybe fifteen years old—there was no way I could go to university at that age. My dad was a dairy man with all these kids—we had the University Dairy out in Richmond. Nursing is very hard for a young girl off the farm. We used to have all these boys come in off the ship and they were being treated for gonorrhea, you know? I didn't know about any of these things. But I learned fast! They were nice boys, and a lot of them couldn't speak much English, so we couldn't converse very well. But you got so you learned, so you could make them comfortable and all that. I learned a lot.

My first ward, when I worked on the floor, was the workers' compensation ward, and we had all these loggers. The tricks they pulled and the things they did! They'd ask for the duck, and I wouldn't know what the duck was! [*Laughs.*] That's the urinal. And they'd go, "Quack! Quack!" I was shy, but it didn't last long. Those boys kept the place going. There was a Sister Francis who was the head of this fourth floor, the compensation ward, and she'd go and cook them steaks and things, you know. She'd be harder than nails with them, but she'd go fix them up a good steak and stuff. Maybe you had to be tough, especially with those fellas. But then you did something so they'd know you cared.

When I was in training as a nurse we didn't have any antibiotics. It was strictly a nursing deal. We were washing and changing morning jackets. That's a soft cloth coat that absorbs the perspiration between the drinks you gave them to bring down the fever. They were perspiring profusely, and you had to keep changing these things and washing their chests and backs because you had to keep the fever down.

It was my last year of training, that would be 1940, and the sulfa drugs came in then. Penicillin was right after. And there were all sorts of jokes going around the hospital. "Have you heard of self-a-denial?" That sort of thing. It was just fabulous, the difference. It took a while to see it. One thing about the sulfa—you always gave it intramuscular at that time—it was hard on the tissues. And another thing, in those days we didn't have disposable needles so we had to take the barbs off the used ones, sort of sharpen them up. If you didn't take care of the needles, well, getting a shot really hurt. So you spent hours doing things like that. Preparation.

We didn't think nurses would be tied up with these things, that there would always be time for personal care. But you see, they [those running hospitals, health services, etc.] depleted the nursing numbers tremendously. On staff and in the field. Public health used to do so much more for the patient than they can do now. Today it's strictly a numbers business.

I think it's been a gradual change. When I worked at Family Rehabilitation, there was a great deal of talk at that time about the "quality of care,"

but it was all theoretical. Family Rehab was doing a tremendous job reha-
bilitating people, but the aides and nursing staff weren't into it at all. I was
supervising. That was difficult, because you couldn't get a nurse; there were
very few of them. They were very busy, and there was so much paperwork.
Mind you, I think some people were in hospitals when they really didn't
need to be.

These are things I learned later in life.

My first husband was in the army and then he was in Shaughnessy Hospital for a long time before his discharge. The war, you know? It meant that
I had to live on the family farm for quite a few years—actually until my son
started school and we could get our own home. I think there's a psychological aspect to it too. Mostly, it started before my husband died. I was working
a full-time job. Even when the children were small, I worked as a nurse. So
after he died, when I looked back at it, I think this Parkinson's disease of his
was already coming on. But I didn't have any idea then. But then, nobody
did. He died in 1968. In 1965, I had taken a year off to go back to school in
nursing administration. I collapsed and went to my husband's doctor, who
was also treating him for a heart condition. He said I had some problems
with my heart. But, you know, I lost weight and did all the things he told me
to, and I still just had more problems. It was pretty rough for a while.

Now, finally, I think I have it all pretty well in hand. But it hasn't been
easy, that's for sure. Not the general loss of self-esteem, not the loss of being
able to get out on your own. After my husband died, instead of using the
time—when my children were gone—I made so many mistakes within just
a few short years. I remarried, and when I look back I should have known I
was going around with the wrong people. I knew better. And I thought I
was having a good time, but I wasted some years. Then I lost my job, and it
wasn't because of anything about my depression. It was my health. I had
two angiograms for my heart. It made me angry, getting let go from my
work, and so I found another job right away, in William's Lake. That's
where I got married again. This fellow was from William's Lake.

I was really furious because I'd lost my husband. I don't care who it is,
when someone dies your whole life changes. Right after, you try to get it
back. Afterwards, it's a different picture altogether. My children were away.
If I had had a little support from them, it would have helped. You know? We
don't look after our people very well anymore.

Anyway, the marriage was a mistake. While I was getting my divorce, I
went up to the Queen Charlottes and worked in the mine there. I was the
only nurse, and there was a doctor, an elderly man, a wonderful person. My

daughter was in Toronto and having problems, which I knew about. I mean, her problems were a big part of my problems too. She phoned me to meet her and the children in Vancouver. So I left my job up north and went to see her.

I liked that job at the mine. I liked working with the doctor and all that. There was no social life, really. There were some very nice people there. But most of them were either alcoholics or drug users, those who stay in those towns. Don't get me wrong; it was an experience I wouldn't want to have missed. It was hard to take the drinking. I don't mean to say I don't take a drink. I do. What I mean, I was a little afraid that I'd take too many drinks myself if I stayed up there.

And then I went back to Toronto with my daughter. I went back east. My daughter says, "The next time you come, Mother, don't bring all your furniture." But what do you do with this stuff? So I put it in storage. Anyway, first I went to Toronto to be with her and then I came back here to Vancouver and got this job in Pleasant Vista. I was matron there and I liked that very much. Now these were all seniors. It was personal care, and I lived right in the building. There were two apartments of resident doctors, but I had to supervise them, too, to see that everyone was okay.

Nursing homes? I wouldn't go there if I was dying. The thing is, you're mixed with people. It's not that I don't like people, I do. But if you're not feeling well yourself, and the person in the next room is sick . . . too bad. And you have to eat at group tables. If they're acting weird, the people at your table, well, it's awfully hard to put up with. When you get older and you don't have to go to work, you don't want to be told to eat breakfast at a certain time, to eat lunch at a certain time, to have to eat whatever they serve. If you want a poached egg, "No way," they say. This sort of thing. You suddenly have freedom from a lot of things, but there's no freedom in a nursing home. And yet, I do think they have to be organized to that extent to handle that many people. I feel they're doing their best.

When I was at Pleasant Vista, one of the relatives had been a classmate of mine. Her mother was there, and she and her husband would come to visit every now and then, but they just upset the mother. They'd always be higher than a kite. I used to get furious, because the patients were nice people and they would be there just alone. Or there would be visitors and they would be . . . upsetting.

I know my own two children, not that they're not good—they're tremendous—but I don't want to be a burden to them in any way. I don't think I ever would be because I don't think they would allow it. I think that's probably my own doing. We try to be very independent. I mean, that's what's within us. It almost goes with our dignity. I think a lot of things are just part of you. You come with a certain makeup. I think the only way I could succeed in my life, the only time that I felt that Mother approved or Dad approved—mostly Mother—was if I was out front. Independent, responsible, you know? It was very competitive, my family. I don't think I'm competitive now, but I still feel that I'd like to be able to do these things myself.

I know I can't do things now, like walk without someone going with me. Still, I'd like to just browse by myself at the library, for example. Good as the people are at the library who help me, they don't have the time to say "hello," hardly. I had meals-on-wheels for a while, and I stopped it because the effort of going to the door and letting them in was too much at that time. Also, they were very, very busy. In and out. Now I have to phone for my groceries. But I do think the services they give us are tremendous. I'm staying right here until I die.

Sometimes, like the groceries, well you have no idea the things they send me. If I could only *look* at those shelves and pick out my own things. The people who shop for me, it's a long-term care service at a volunteer, long-term care organization. Volunteers phone you and get your order. They phone me on Sunday mornings, which I don't like, and it's delivered Tuesday. They phone you first to tell you how much it is, so you'll have your check ready. You think you've given careful instructions about what you want, and what you end up with—because it goes through three people before the store—it's like the poached egg at the nursing home. Either you don't get it, or you get two dozen.

Actually, I could go shopping on Thursdays with a volunteer buddy from Senior Care. That's a volunteer organization here. But it's a different place they go to each Thursday in that program so you still don't know where everything is in the store, what's on which shelf, you know? I haven't availed myself of it yet, because I haven't felt up to it. Also, they've offered I can go to, it used to be called St. Michael's, once or twice a week. It's a nursing home, but they have services there, too. I remember when it was built and going to see it when it opened. Anyway, you go for three hours and have your lunch. But that doesn't appeal to me at all. I'm just not ready for that yet.

Now this friend of mine who died last year, we were very close. She fought right to the end. She wasn't going! It wasn't that she was afraid to die or anything like that. But she drove her car right up to the last few months, that kind of thing. And she was always sort of the leader, although her energy got lower and lower in those months. We still went every week, maybe five of us, to her house. She was a pianist as well. She had two great big pianos, grand pianos, in her living room. She did some of the music teaching for a college here. She was seventy-seven and she fought her illness every step. Yes, she did. I always think of the younger ones, they've got so much to live for. Now Mabel felt she had something to live for, too. She must have.

I was really feeling terrible recently. After you talked to me and asked for this interview, I said to myself, "Maybe I am good for something. Maybe I am needed some way." When I had the nervous breakdown, I felt my kids would be better off if I were gone. I still get those feelings sometimes. The doctor always says my heart goes wonky when I feel like that. And afterwards I'm terribly tired. After we talked on the phone, you and me, I was psychologically up because I knew I could be of some use. Being needed, some way, that's what it is.

My one granddaughter went to Toronto to start school. She's going into fashion marketing. I miss her terribly because I don't see her that often any more. And then I have another granddaughter in Calgary who's the same age. And I have one grandson who is having a very bad time in life. They've said he's schizophrenic. I don't like the labels. Not that he couldn't be. He could. But he's up in Whitehorse and I'd like to see him get a proper evaluation. He just had a birthday and I wrote to him and talked to him on the phone. He was in hospital. He was in jail on his birthday last year in Kamloops. Had a wonderful time, he said.

In my home I can manage very well, and I have a homemaker who comes in. I couldn't do without her. She has to help me with my bath and everything like that. That's very hard on older people, hard getting used to needing help with things like that. But now that I'm used to her coming in, I don't think anything about it. My daughter had several parties at her place when her daughter was going away and quite a few people came back here. I enjoyed that so much because a lot of them were people I'd known over the years. One of the other outings I have these days is funerals. It's nice to see everybody! That's the way it gets, I think.

My daughter is alone now, you see. It's the first time that her children are gone. When she was in trouble, she separated from her husband—which was a very good thing. And she's been alone since, with her two children. She called me last night and said, "Would you like to go up to Hope [*a small British Columbia town*] and see Auntie Margaret?" That's my youngest sister. And I said, "Oh, I'd really love it." And she asked, "Do you think you can manage?" I said, "I'll do just fine. I'll have to stop along the way and have a cup of coffee or cup of tea or something, but other than that I'll do just fine." So if the weather is all right, we're going. But she's very busy, very busy. And the other granddaughter, she's moved in with her boyfriend—that's what they do these days. So I guess she's busy too.

I'm a real fussbudget. If Sharon [*the home aide*] can't come, I tell Audrey [*the supervisor*], "Send somebody I know. Not a stranger." Just the thought of having a stranger come and having to be helped by her into the tub and out of the tub, that sort of thing . . . it's uncomfortable, you know? It's almost like the nurse's position in the hospital. Most patients will take to a nurse they know doing things that would be embarrassing otherwise. These homemakers, particularly the one I have, she has male patients with amputations that have to be bathed and different things like that. And she's able to put them at ease. She's doing what we used to do. She listens, and we discuss all these things quite a bit. I think her role is tremendous.

Some of my neighbors say, "Why do you have a homemaker? Why does your doctor come to the house?" They think this is costing them a lot of money in, you know, in taxes. I mean, I pay for my homemaker but still, it's subsidized. I don't pay the whole thing. My doctor said, "You say to them, 'Well, it's saving a lot of money because to be treated in a hospital costs so much more.'" The woman who came to the door just now while we were talking, for example, she's older than me. And her husband has been very ill with emphysema. She has a homemaker come in. But her income is much higher than mine, so she has to pay more. And I won't discuss with her how much I pay, which makes her furious.

I like my things around me. I like to be home. Most of the time I feel I'm so very lucky because I can be in my own home. I knit, knit, knit. I used to do a lot of volunteer work, but now I can't get out to do it. So I knit. I think I've done twelve afghans since May. [*Laughs.*] And there are more on the way. They go to my grandchildren and to the four of us who lived together after we graduated high school. My friends. I made one for each of them at the end of May. A lady who used to be a neighbor comes in to do reflexology. We trade—I give her an afghan. I think that's part of the thing that I would like to feel, that my neighbors didn't think I was a pain in the neck, a burden.

I don't know why it's gotten to this point. It gets me angry, inasmuch as home care is a service that we have found that we need. I would never want to go back to the way it was for my parents—they had to pay for everything in medicine. And I paid my taxes for many, many years. I'd been nursing pretty well from 1941 until I had to retire. I raised my two children, looked after my homes—had several of them—looked after my mother. But I think what they're trying to infer is that I'm now a burden.

It's not a financial issue. People try to make out that this is about money but it's not. It's about being myself. About being me. And I had to learn to be me after fifty. A United Church counselor said that was the only thing that was wrong, that was causing my depressions. I had to be able to find out who "me" was. That's why I use the name "Holly" rather than "Mrs. Treeson." Because I'm Holly! And I'm glad that's straightened out. Sometimes it slips, like any of these things do, but I've been lucky. I've learned this much at least.

The library comes once a month. I have a lot of programs on TV. My friend Mabel, who died, got me introduced to a lot of musical things. And she'd call me in the middle of the night and ask me about something she was reading. She'd keep my interest going all the time. Now there's nobody to discuss anything with.

I have one friend who is ten years younger than me. You know, sometimes I pass out. They think it's the heart. Poof, like that. Twice she was with me when this happened. You call the ambulance, they come and put the oxygen on, I'm sort of groggy for quite a while, and sometimes I have to stay in the hospital. The last time I had one of these attacks was last November, and I asked for a complete neurological deal because I'd once been [*erroneously*] treated for Parkinson's.

I look forward to the next time I'll see my son and his wife—he has a new wife, a Swedish girl. I just love them. I only see him a couple times a year. And I look forward to seeing my daughter very much, too. She tries to keep in touch at least once a week. Other than that, since my relatives went, it's been very hard. I still want to make ties, but it's just harder to meet people. I do have two very good friends who were part of Mabel's group from the college and they both drive. They're always anxious to take me places, but this summer hasn't been good. I mean, my health hasn't been good this summer. And they're busy too. They have families, both of them. I really look forward to going out with them. I've had a poor summer. I don't do well in the heat.

I'm very envious of people whose partners last with them, I think it's wonderful for them. Especially if they've grown together instead of apart. I see it in some older people. The couple at the end of the hall in this building, she developed Alzheimer's. And he looked after her until she had to be placed, and he then went every day and fed her. And you know, he's the one person in the building who will phone me when he's around and say, "Is there anything you need?"

It's nice to see people doing that, caring. We're not all bad. I think we have to go through things before we learn to live, to appreciate what we have. That's why I say, I feel so lucky so often. When I was a nurse, I was often amazed that people could suffer such terrible losses and come right up again. Some, not all of them by any means. But it's surprising, I think, that most did.

The doctor tells me that loneliness adds to physical problems. I have real physical problems—it's not all in my head. You see, I've had quite a few breaks from the osteoporosis. Fortunately I'm not in pain all the time. But I have to remember that when I am in pain, if my thoughts get down, I tell myself to accept life. I try to handle it better. I also find myself reading things about diet. That helps—all these things that may come into it. I read a lot. I have to be in control. I haven't always been, so I'm making up for it now.

I think we should give some thought to educating people that old age doesn't mean you don't have the same desires, you don't have the same needs—which I suppose is the same thing—that you had when you were much younger. You do. You have the freedom, but you also need the sharing. That's sometimes the hardest to find. I want to share my thoughts, but nobody wants to listen. And that's why I miss my friends so much. My one sister-in-law here, in Vancouver, I could pick up the phone and call her, whatever was troubling me. And she was the same. She could always call me. And you know, it wouldn't be such a big problem then, because I was able to share it with someone. And the same with something nice that you want to share.

As we get older, we still have lots of thoughts. I am very political, for example. I want to hear everything everyone says, and I have thoughts about what they say. And about these commentators on TV or radio. I definitely wasn't a person as far as my mother was concerned, or my family. My brother who's just a year older than I, the one who is left, he was a brewmaster. He went as far as he could go, and I was at the top of my profession as well. The others were very jealous of that. But you work very hard for those things.

I don't know what other families are like, but I don't encourage anyone to have a big family because I don't think there's enough time to spend with each one person in the family. I had two older brothers, and we were all just a year apart. Being the girl, I helped Mother. These days, you know, I like to see these young women who take over. I'm not a feminist, but I like the trend very much. I'm not a male-basher either. In fact, I like men. In the administration I dealt with a lot of men, but I think they need a little more, ah, understanding of what their role is, more humanity. The women, I think, they have it.

Not all men or all women are one way or the other, of course. Dad's father lived a long life. He ended up in a Salvation Army home, doing the cooking. He must have been in his seventies. The other grandfather was this great big tall Swedish man, and he got more Swedish in his accent as he went along. He lived into his seventies, too. He died in the general hospital, where they have the older people.

Me? Well, I'll have to live to 2003 to pay my mortgage out. I don't want to leave any bills behind me. Then I'll go on a trip. It's good when you get to my age or my mother's age. She had a bad turn about five years before she died, and we thought she was going then. It was quite a bad time. But she was bound and determined—one of her great-grandchildren was pregnant, and she was going to see that baby. Well, she lived to see that baby and then the third or the fourth.

I think it's my family background—I couldn't see why all this business of getting old was so important. Just as long as the doctor keeps me comfortable, I'm all for it. If I have to have surgery on my back or something, I will. They've suggested that already, but Dr. Bill and I decided to wait and see how mobile I could keep myself. My daughter and I are trying to get into a more spiritual life. Then you don't have a horror of death, but you still have a feeling of wanting to live.

I had a death experience after one of my surgeries, and after that I was not afraid to die. I came close to it quite a few times. I'm not afraid to die, like some people who have terrible fears of dying. It's pretty shattering to see people really suffering. The problem is, there's been no proper planning for it. We're living much longer, and we simply have to prepare for it. We can't let them be on the street.

POSTSCRIPT

One of Holly Treeson's knitted afghans sits on the sofa in my living room in winter. A deep, rust brown, it is, she said one day, "my color." It arrived the week after she died unexpectedly, after emergency abdominal surgery. Her doctor called to tell me, and to tell me, too, how important I had been to her in her final years.

She had cared for others, cared for her mother. Now, however, the only people who cared for her were volunteers from social service agencies, an aide paid for by the provincial health service, and a friendly physician who listened to her views and concerns. After the death of her old friend Mabel, a grievous loss, she had no way to replace that association. Her children and grandchildren were far away and, like Alex Sarnoff, she knew a closer association would be burdensome to them.

She was lonely but not embittered. She did not want to die, only to live more fully; to increase associations with people of her past and present. In this context, my visits became progressively important. When I was away from Vancouver we talked perhaps once a week. Over the period of a year or so her relations with her daughter degenerated. She didn't understand, Holly said. Her daughter was impatient and demanding and rude. We talked about it endlessly and usually without resolution. Eventually, Holly asked if I would be her will's executor. She didn't trust her family, with whom she was feuding, and wanted someone who "knows me as I am." I discussed this with Bill McArthur, who was worried he had drawn me into a complex family dynamic. "Remember," he said in one conversation, "she doesn't want you, she wants her children to want her. That's what this is about."

And so I provisionally agreed to do what she asked if she would meet a few conditions. Before she changed her will I asked her to write down the things she would want me to do, the things most important to her. I asked her also to write a letter to her children explaining why she had asked me to take on this task. And while she was at it, I suggested, why not put in the letter what her hopes and disappointments had been. In short, I gave her chores I hoped would help her perceive that what she wanted was a closer relationship with her family and not with me.

It worked. The task of writing—"I need a record of this, Holly. Dr. Bill agrees a written letter is best"—gave her time to collect her thoughts. In our discussions she would read me a paragraph and we would then discuss it. All this helped her understand that she was indeed angry that nobody cared for her as she had cared for others in her life. Eventually she called to say that she and her daughter had a "good talk" and that she was comfortable with not changing her will. She was concerned, however, that I'd feel betrayed, left out. "After all," she said, "you've done so much. I don't want you to be angry now." I assured her that what I wanted was what would be best for her.

Five or six days later Bill McArthur called to tell me she had died. Ten days after our last conversation the afghan—"I have a surprise coming for you," she had said—arrived in the mail. With it was a note that said, simply, "Thanks. I love you. Holly." On winter nights I wrap it about me and sit in my rocker while watching the snow.

NOTE

1. Through the first half of this century, nurses were typically trained by hospitals, and especially Catholic hospitals, and not in university programs. See Daniel F. Chambliss, *Beyond Caring: Hospitals, Nurses, and the Social Organization of Ethics* (Chicago: University of Chicago Press, 1996), 72.

5

The Teenage Bride

More than fifty years ago I could perceive for myself that the race is not always to the swift nor the battle to the strong, but that time and chance happen to us all.

Joseph Heller, *God Knows*

Tina and Tim Harding exemplify the type of couple that Holly Treeson envied, people who have grown together over the years. At the time of this interview Tina was seventy-two years old, five years her husband's junior. Mr. Harding demonstrates many of the symptoms of advancing Parkinson's disease: occasional confusion, emotional depression, a "crying voice" resulting from the disease's effects on the vocal cords, and a progressive muscular weakness. Like most Parkinsonians, his face is slightly waxen and fixed, giving him a slightly "grumpy" appearance.

They lived together in suburban Honolulu where she was his "primary caregiver," assisting him in his restricted life. On one level she exemplifies the old-style wife who lives for her husband, whose job is and has been nurturing and caring. It was only later, in his interview, that a broader perspective developed of her, him, and their life together.

I was about thirteen years old when I met Tim, but I started to go with him when I was fourteen and I was married when I was not quite seventeen. I never had another boyfriend. To me he was like a father figure. He was like a brother. In fact, he looked a lot like my older brother, whom I adore. And he was everything. He was so bright! He would tell me about the stars and things that I didn't know because I had just started high school and he was going to college. We went with each other for two years and we were married and we've been married fifty-six years. I thought everybody did that: got married and stayed married. It never occurred to me that it could be otherwise. I always said, "If Timmy didn't marry me, I don't know who would."

Timmy, I think, still sees me as sixteen. Whenever we were in a department store, even when he was well, if he didn't like what I was saying to him, he'd say, "Tina!" and everyone would turn around and ask, "Who is Tina? A little baby?" I am seventy-two! He still thinks of me as sixteen. If I tell him to do something, most of the time, now, I'm right. I feel sorry for him. I think of him as a young man. I see him the same. He doesn't look any older to me. I think he looks the same. I feel sorry that he can't walk. I can't believe it, because he would always be walking ahead of me as if we were from another culture . . . men in front, you know? He walked so fast. Now I feel badly. I would rather it had happened to me. To me, he's always the same. He knows that I've grown a lot. He really raised me. There was a time I wouldn't talk about that [*death*]. Now, I don't think I'm afraid anymore. I don't want to go, I don't want to leave. I like it here. I like it here with Tim, no matter what.

I never wanted to go. I don't want the hereafter. I want it all right now. I want to see real people and real things. I sort of feel, well, I've always been afraid of death. Recently I lost a friend of thirty-some years. She played tennis and just dropped on the tennis court. She was seventy-six. Tim just asked me—I just had a little dizzy spell—and he said, "You haven't told me what you want done if you black out." And I said, "Just let me lie there." I was joking, of course. But right now I've sort of given up, because it's hard to watch someone you love very much deteriorate, to see someone who was so independent become dependent. And who cries, you know?

I've been married for fifty-six years, and I would not hurt my husband and start an argument with him and stand up for my so-called rights at this time because at this time it's very important that he still knows he is the man of the house. People usually treat him like, "Oh, that senile old invalid," and my husband is not like that. He's seventy-seven, but he has a better figure than most men at forty, and his mind is—you've spoken to him, so you know—his mind is excellent. He remembers everything. If I need a telephone number, I don't go looking it up in my records. It's, "Tim, what is that number we had, when, in 1963?" And he'll still know it by heart.

We grew up in the times when women did not expect to be equal to men. They didn't want to be. They realized the man had a hard time. He had to work, and his lot in life was that he had to support his wife and family. At that time, you didn't think of a career for yourself. So we gave him his due—at least I did. I loved him very much. Also, he's five years older than I am. He was in college and I was in high school when we were first together. If he told me the moon was black I would have believed him. I thought he was so bright. I was the only girl in my high school who had a fellow going to St. John's University. I never had a high school boyfriend. I knew he was smart. I always told him he was smart, and he said that he wasn't smart until he met me.

People treat him differently now because he walks with a cane. Yes, they do. Sometimes his voice breaks when he talks, which is part of Parkinson's. The voice goes. He's not crying, but it sounds like he's crying. If he gets excited and wants to tell you something, his voice breaks. My husband is not an invalid. He's just sick and not feeling well, and he knows it. And he's upset about it. He gets cranky because of that. With Parkinson's, you have to be patient. There really isn't too much you can do. It isn't death immediately, so you can't do too much for it. Also, he's introverted by nature. He's not an "up" man, never was. I am the only one who really gives him . . . I'm his slave. I'm his mother. I'm his girlfriend. I'm his wife. I'm his, ah, nurse. Not really. He has a nurse. He doesn't want me to be his nurse. He doesn't want me to help him with a bath. He doesn't want me to help him dress. He barely likes me to even touch him. He wants to be The Husband, just as he's always been. He has been very satisfied with his life up to now, and I think even now he keeps saying how lucky we are that we live in Hawaii and that we retired to a nice place and have enough income to live comfortably. And that we are together.

Each day is another day. There are days when Tim will get up in the morning and say, "Let's go." He loves to go for the ride around the Windward Mall. He loves the little island near Sea Life Marine Park, the island in the middle of Kaneohe Bay. He thinks that's the most beautiful spot in the whole world. He loves the ridged mountains behind our house, and I do too. Usually we'll get into the car about ten o'clock. He uses a cane because he can't walk too far. He's lucky if he does half a block. He doesn't seem to want to go out walking anymore. He says he can't. He does have trouble with rheumatism and other things.

I don't like to drive at night anymore because I'm on medication for my heart and for high blood pressure. I don't wear glasses when I drive, but my eyesight isn't too good. I don't know if it's on account of my age. Tim won't sit in the car when I drive, however, even though I've never had a citation and have driven for a long time. It makes him very nervous when I drive. So when we go out, well, he drives. We go to the Kahala Hilton. We had an account there for years. And to Hickham Officers Club. But now, lately, we haven't been doing even that. I'll dash over to the local movie if there is something I want to see.

A bad day is a day he feels everything is gone. He's lost everything. He eats, thank goodness, if I give him the food. He has to have the same thing every day, always the same food. And he will not take even a glass of water himself. If I leave, I guess he'll have to. My daughter says, "Mother, he'll eat. If he's hungry, he'll eat." But he likes me to do the feeding. So a bad day is sitting around. I give him his breakfast, and then I'll dash out to the store and buy a few things. When I come in, he's sleeping. He sleeps most of the time. If he's not happy, he sleeps. But then he stays up at night. He'll look at his TV programs and go to sleep later. So that when he wakes up in the morning, he isn't really rested. He'll eat his breakfast and have to go to sleep again.

I have two people helping. One is a nurse's aide and I was happy to get her because you can't let just anyone take care of Tim. He prefers a nice young girl, and we have one now. She comes at 7:30. I leave to take my walk. Sometimes he'll walk with her, just about ten minutes of walking for him.[1] That's it. Then she gives him his shower, and they have a cup of coffee and he's happy. He would be happy, I think, if I could have her come every day for a couple of hours. Would I be, too? Yes. There's never been jealousy in our marriage. I don't know what that means because I've never had another boyfriend—he's never given me any reason. And if he tells me he's been out with someone, I say, "Great, as long as you had a good time. As long as it doesn't cost me anything."

Even just the two days a week that this young lady comes to visit, they have helped me so much. She gives him a shower and he tells her stories. She's really interested because this is all new to her. He knows all about Asia. He knows all about Europe. People who have never heard his stories are just fascinated by them. Most everyone likes him. The ladies like him because he tells them tales. And they're very good stories. It's helped me so much having her here. I feel relieved that he's up. He feels good. He'll dress and he'll talk, and he's happy when he's stimulated.

Before the Parkinson's, seven years ago, the doctor found he had a tumor on his brain. My oldest son came over from California and we did the operation right away. We were lucky and it wasn't malignant. But then there are these other things. And right now he worries he might get another tumor. Yesterday, he went for a CAT scan. I did not want him to go for a CAT scan, because if it was another tumor, I would not want him to have another operation. He's seventy-seven. If he doesn't know about it, fine. Myself, I will not go for a mammogram. My friend had one and she dropped dead anyway. She had a mastectomy at the age of seventy-five. I thought it was wrong to do that. No way, I don't want it.

He's had so many problems with the doctors, you wouldn't believe. The reason he found out he had a brain tumor was he went to the internist and they told him to get a GI [gastro-intestinal] series. They treated him as if he was a hypochondriac. He had the brain tumor all the time and nobody even suggested a CAT scan. So he went for this test for a GI series or something like that, and they did not send his chart down to say what he was allergic to. He was on medication of different kinds, for high blood pressure, for other things, and he had no idea they hadn't sent his chart down. They gave him this drug or something and Timmy had a stroke! At least, they thought it was a stroke. But it didn't look like a stroke—he knew where he was and everything.[2] They decided they wanted to keep him in hospital overnight. As they were taking him upstairs, I said, "He just came in for that GI series; I can't understand it." Then I found out they had given him some sort of drug he was allergic to because they didn't even have his chart. So Dr. K said, "Gee, Tim. I didn't know."

The stress is not being able to do what I want. It isn't Tim's fault either. He has to have someone to tell, "I don't feel well. I feel dizzy." At the same time, he needs to be motivated. He needs to have people to talk to, the same type of people as he is. He's tired of seeing just me around all the time. I don't think he's tired of seeing me, but he wants to do what he wants to do. He takes over the whole house. That's stressful for me! I'm not the best housekeeper in the world, but I like my things in order. I want papers to be put away, and Tim says when I put them away we—he—can never find them. Which is true. He puts them away, he finds them, but then they're all over the house. And you dare not touch one of those papers. It's not my house anymore. It used to be the opposite. "Oh no, you're not doing that to my new table. Take it up to your den or your room or I'm going to throw it out." Well, I don't say that anymore.

I get so mad that I'll go up and . . . I have to cry quietly. He's angry if I cry. He cries all the time, but I'm not supposed to. And he gets very upset if I'm upset. If I get angry, he feels like I'm letting him down. That I just don't want to talk. It's not like me to not want to talk. So I feel like I can't get angry too often. But what I do is sing a little song, and he knows I'm mad if I'm humming a little tune when he tells me something. Really, it's part of Parkinson's, part of the disease—they're grumpy. They do not smile. Well, I don't remember Timmy smiling too much anyway. He's not that type of person. But he has a very good sense of humor, and if we have people over, in the house, he interacts. And he loves it. He has a subtle sense of humor. So I always have to explain, "He doesn't mean that." Being grumpy, crying. But I've done that all my life, explained things so people don't get insulted.

After my heart attack he was a little more careful of me. They told me it was stress. But I really was overweight. And I had cholesterol, which I never knew because I swam two hours a day. I'm a swimmer and, well, it's only the last two years since I had the heart attack that I don't swim. I walk six miles a day, but I don't swim very much anymore because the pool we have in our townhouse complex is not heated. The cardiologist asked me if the pool was heated and when I said no he said, "I'd prefer you walk. You can swim, but be sure, you know, that it isn't a shock." I must say my walking has helped me a great deal. Since the heart attack I've learned to live alone. I've learned to take a walk by myself. I'd rather have girlfriends along, or Tim with me, but I do it myself. And I feel lonely. I feel like no one cares for him but me.

Actually, I'm glad when five o'clock comes. I do what I did with my children. After five o'clock, I'm nobody's mother. Tim's used to it, and he seems relieved. He gets to sit downstairs on the couch with his television. He likes different programs than ladies do—I like talk shows; he likes war pictures. So I go upstairs. I have a television upstairs in my bedroom. And I'll take in my show, maybe write a postcard or something if I want to, and just relax. I can look at my television. I call down, "Are you all right?" He's had everything I can possibly give him. And I just stay up there.

I think he feels angry. I think he feels angry at me because . . . I think he's angry because I had a heart attack. I'm not supposed to be sick. I never was sick. I'm supposed to be there for him. Otherwise, he calls "Tina!" and I hop. It's not scary because I know Tim. I know he loves me very much. And I know if he talks to anybody he can't stop bragging about me. He can't say, "I love you. You look beautiful." He used to say it as we were growing up. But this is hard for him now. It's hard for him to say, "I'm sorry." I never put him in that position. He cannot say it. I can say, "I'm sorry," even when I'm not sorry, just to make him feel good. I say, "I'm sorry. I was wrong." It doesn't bother me to say I was wrong even when I know I was right.

You asked about our children. Our oldest son, who is now fifty, is a California city councilman and a vice-mayor. He was born in 1939. Our second son was born in 1944. Our third son was born in 1950, and our daughter was born in 1956. You can see I had an active life! [*Laughs.*] Every time I sent one off to school, I had another baby. So each baby was like an only child. There was no birth control pill at that time. We used our own birth control. Nobody told us what to do, but we knew, we knew. We didn't have children for the first five years. We said we wouldn't. I worked as a saleslady in a department store. Tim worked for the government and went to school at night. We transferred to Washington, D.C., lived there. Lived in Virginia. We lived almost every place in the country. And we had our children spaced apart. Nobody told us how to do that.

My oldest son is very concerned about Tim. He's our firstborn and he's very, very much attached to his dad and to me. He'll call, and he's very much involved and wants Tim to get the right pills. You know. Our oldest son calls at least two or three times a week and he's been wonderful. And that's all Tim really wants. All he wants is to be respected, as he was before. He's a proud man.

Craig, the second son, was here about two years ago. He's a "yuppie," the vice-president of a hospital, and now he is almost angry at me. He says, "You don't have to do this. He needs supervised care, and you should give it to him." And he says, "I see people who give up the rest of their life and they're dead and the Parkinson's patient is still alive."

My third son is angry at his dad. Donald was here last year and it wasn't a successful visit. He adopted a boy and he just acts like no one else has ever had a baby. It's his *boy*! He's compensating, I think. Donald wants to be sure that we love his son as much as we love the other grandchildren. Timmy wasn't feeling well when they visited and wanted Donald to take care of his little boy by himself because it was right after my heart attack. Tim thought I was overworking for them, but didn't realize I was doing the same for him.

Well, Donald visited and he watched me. This was after a heart attack about two years ago. He watched me, and he thought I was doing too much. Tim said, "Did the paper arrive today?" and I said, "Oh, my God, I forgot to bring it in." And Donald, who is a professor at the University of California, said, "Do you mean you fetch his paper every morning? Why doesn't he take a walk out there and get it?" "Well," I said, "Donald, it isn't because he's ill. I've fetched his paper since before you were even dreamed of. About fifty-six years ago I fetched the paper! I don't resent doing that."

I get angry with them. In California, they're busy taking me out places, but they're never interested in going out with their dad. Even though he takes nothing from anybody, I feel they would be so happy if it was over. Even when they call, they're speaking with me. They seem to be angry that he's sick. It's "Is Mom coming to visit?" or they're coming to visit *me*. And Mom has other things to do. I feel the less they see of us, the better. Now it's not fun anymore when they come. It isn't as easy. Now that they're married and work, they don't just pick up and go. If Mother sends the ticket, they can. But I don't think they want to come. I think they're hurt, they're mad because he's sick. It's not that they don't love him, I'm sure that they do. How could you not love a father? He was good to them, and, you know, took them everyplace and did everything a father should do for them. He was a strict father, though.

With our daughter May, we feel differently. She's the baby. She's just thirty-four years old. We're happy she's married and seems to have a good marriage. She has two little children, one is four and one is three. She lives over here on the North Shore of Oahu, and it's a two and a half hour drive from here. My daughter does not come to visit too often. She's not very sympathetic. Her husband is a doctor and he thinks Tim could do a lot of things for himself. Actually, I love it that she's married. When you have three sons, you want them to be good citizens—and they are, and they're happy. But with a daughter, even though she has a husband who can care for her and she seems happy and she has two children, you still feel very connected, very much connected. You feel responsible, regardless. But she's not sympathetic at all.

It seems awful, but you think you know your children and you really don't. I didn't raise them that way. We feel like there's no soul, there's no feeling of responsibility in them. Responsibility isn't the word I mean. It's compassion. That's what they don't have. It makes me angry at the children because I feel they should give him more attention and sympathy for being a father who has been a good dad and a loyal dad. I feel that we're old people now. We're a burden. We're not a burden financially, and we live far away. But we're a burden because they feel guilty.

I think Tim likes it better when we're alone, and they resent this for me. The first thing my third boy said about Tim's illness was, "Oh, Mother. Now you can come back to Long Beach and live. All your friends are here. You can come back and buy an apartment, a condominium." We lived there before coming to Hawaii, you know. And I said no, Tim does not want to live in Long Beach anymore. He likes Hawaii. And my son said, "Well, that's too bad. But you certainly can." And I said, "But what will I do with Tim?" And he said, "That's his problem." This is the third boy, and these are very bright children. And they were brought up with a loving father who was

Cub Scout master and started Boy Scout groups for them and everything. They seem to resent the fact that I am going away from them.

They're kids. I feel that they are immature. You must remember each one was brought up at a different time period. If you think of a son who was brought up in 1939, you know why he is so attached and why he is so caring. Then think of a son who was born in 1944, who was brought up in the 1950s and 1960s. And then think of another who was born in 1950. And so, they are the generation that is immature. Also, they're selfish. They've had everything. They've had cars, education. Our four children together have twelve degrees, so you know Timmy must have done something right!

I don't want their help. I really wouldn't put it on them. Neither would Tim. He wouldn't want that. We don't want anyone to help us. As long as I'm alive, Timmy is going to be fine. I always handled the finances. He was an accountant. But he couldn't count anything under a million dollars, so he never worried about the money. If I gave him a dollar for lunch, fine. In fact, he can't even believe what I've done. If I'm not around—I have told my daughter and I put it in writing—she will be the guardian. She will get the complete estate, whatever we have. Tim's income goes on as long as he lives. He has three pensions. He worked for the government for thirty-six years, and then he has a company pension, and he has Social Security. And if anything happens to me, my daughter knows that all you have to do with Tim is get him a nice young girl to drive the car, prepare the food, and he can pay her as much—or more—to take good care of him. And he'll be fine.

"Come to California," they tell me. "Why can't you get up and go! You're able to travel if you want to, anytime." But it's no longer that much of a pleasure to travel alone. And even when I did travel alone before, I never worried what Tim was doing at home, because I knew he could take care of himself.

The friends we had here were in the travel business with us. That was what we did after Timmy retired. We took our travel agent certificates together after Tim retired from the military. Pan Am sent us to London. I was the mouth and he was the brain of the business. We went to school in London, all paid for by the airlines. At one time they did that. We went to Caribbean Cruise. We did so many things and we've done them all together. When you said Tim, it was Tim and Tina.

Now my friends are angry for me. They feel I should be getting out more, doing things more. These aren't bosom buddies. They're people we met here. We'd take them to the Officers Club, which they loved. These were business associates; they weren't personal friends like we had in California.

Mostly my friends there were lady friends. In California, the friends I made were with the children, parents of my children's friends. My children were growing up most of my life, so I had one in high school, one in college, one in junior high, and the baby. And with each child as they grew up, I had a different set of friends. I had friends in preschool of my daughter who once had dated my oldest son! And I did all my socializing there, too: I was PTA president, and I would belong to garden clubs. We never had close friends together because we were mostly friends with each other. Tim was never much of a person to have many friends. I am the one who had the friends. Tim never did. We never had friends we couldn't live without. We had each other.

And now it's just the two of us. I don't have that kind of girlfriend here. My friends were mostly in Long Beach, so they would come here to visit. They would come over, but I no longer invite them because the house is taken over by Tim. He's sitting in his pajamas, his papers in a heap in the living room. It's a small townhouse. It's hard. I feel this is hard. I feel I need to find something else to do. And I can. I can get a job, I can do a million things. But who will take care of him? Now, it's like leaving a child at home. You'd have a guilty feeling. What is he doing? Did he fall down? Can he get up? Is he eating? And he does not take a glass of water unless I give it to him. As I was leaving this afternoon to meet you, he said, "You know I feel so thirsty, I could die. Do you suppose I could have a drink of something?" Well, I went to the refrigerator and got him a Coke.

It's hard for people to understand how you feel, how badly you feel for someone who is deteriorating. It's a very difficult thing to watch. I think he's afraid to be alone. Even when I go away for only three or four days, he's so happy when I return. He's never stood in my way. He won't say I can't. But I think he's scared. I'm scared, too. I'm afraid he might fall, that something might happen to him. I don't want that. I want him to live to be 150 years old. I'll be 145.

POSTSCRIPT

I met Mrs. Harding at a seminar for caregivers hosted by one of Hawaii's major health care suppliers, Kaiser Permanente. She was almost painfully eager to "share" her experiences with others. It was as if she believed that, finally, among others like her, she could argue both her husband's case and her own. She seemed to possess an almost overwhelming need to make others see what their children could not: that Mr. Harding was worth the trouble. Despite his illnesses he was a valuable man and that as his caregiver she was worthy, too.

Her need to talk was so acute that she dominated any attempts at group dialogue and was thus something of a trial to the seminar's organizers. They had hoped to discuss practical issues of elder care. It was an introductory session, not an encounter group or a counseling session. Later, Tina Harding was gently discouraged from participating in a follow-up meeting that Kaiser Permanente offered. She was, instead, encouraged to join a caregiver support group or consider counseling, options she chose to decline. She was, in fact, hurt by what she saw as their rejection, offended by the suggestion she might need counseling, and thus refused any formal help.

From her perspective, neither her children nor their acquaintances understood the closeness—emotional, psychological, historical—that bound her to her husband. To her, their children's desire to entertain her and not Tim Harding was a suggestion that she abandon both her husband and the world they had shared for years. She knew the limits of her world, the constraints of her caring role. But while she would have liked a broader environment, Tina would not purchase it at the price of her husband's comfort. Clearly, to understand her and her life it was necessary to meet Mr. Harding, to find the man behind the complex portrait she painted of a bright, somewhat demanding, rigid accountant with Parkinson's disease.

After our first interview, I talked to Mrs. Harding several times a week. We met on occasion for coffee and I enjoyed her company immensely. Each time I asked if I might visit her husband she would say it was not a "good day." Mr. Harding was feeling ill, he was tired—there was always some excuse. Finally, one Saturday, he answered the phone when I called—"Ah, the boyfriend," he said—and immediately invited me to visit. He looked forward, he said, to a new face and some company.

Her descriptions of her husband did not prepare me for this encounter. He was more and less than she had described. He was clearly a Parkinsonian. He walked carefully, balance toward the balls of his feet. His voice sounded like it was crying whenever he became excited. He warned me about it on our first meeting and seemed to think it a disturbing trait, perhaps unmanly. When it became clear I saw this as at worst a very minor inconvenience, he became quite garrulous and, as Mrs. Harding predicted, I found him an interesting and self-aware man with excellent stories. The next narrative, not surprisingly, is his.

NOTES

1. Walking as a supervised, therapeutic activity is especially important for Parkinson's patients. To maintain mobility as long as possible, it becomes a conscious exercise usually done with another who can protect the person from a fall.

2. If the patient is aware and oriented, the likelihood that it was a stroke, which affects brain functioning, is greatly diminished.

6

The Coward

The past is not a peaceful landscape lying there behind
me . . . As I was moving forward, it was crumbling.
Simone de Beauvoir, *The Coming of Age*

In their living room is a collection of beer steins that serve Tim Harding as a mnemonic. Each reminds him of a hotel where he purchased or "borrowed" the glass; for every stein there is the memory of a country and the assignment that brought him there. Looking fondly at the rows of empty beer steins, each with a crest or hotel name on its front, he recalls the taste of that region's beer. It is a drink he once loved. On some assignments he traveled with his wife and occasionally with his children. Others represent solitary journeys. As a group, they symbolize the complex relation between professional and personal, emotional and practical, that characterizes his life and life view.

Tim Harding's description of his life—professional and personal—offers a complex balance to his wife's narrative. He is not a simple chauvinistic tyrant after all. Where she was proud of him, he is lavish in his praise of her. It was a very proud Mr. Harding who informed me of his wife's business acumen, praised her ability to meet people and develop friends, acknowledged her role in caring for him. Her narrative's view of their children is expanded and critiqued by his understandings, his regrets.

The interview with Mr. Harding was complicated by the couple's tendency to either speak, one for the other, or for one to pause and ask the spouse to complete an idea or supply a name. At first, Mr. Harding said he wanted to be alone with me and suggested his wife leave us when the interview began. He soon called her back to ask her opinion on issues of mutual interest. So, although the narrative was Mr. Harding, his wife's comments, solicited by him, are included in the text as well. After fifty-six years of marriage, each has become an indivisible part of the other. Their stories are intertwined, and he was most comfortable telling it with her present, as participant, audience, and prompter.

My life was so varied. I did so many things in so many capacities. I worked in the Orient for four years—Southeast Asia. I lived in Germany for two years and traveled throughout Europe. I've worked for so many agencies: the army, the navy, the air force, the Department of Defense, and four separate parts of the Treasury Department! I can't look back at any particular job and relive the days. The only thing that I *can* re-live is the time I spent in Vietnam.

All my life I've thought of myself as being more or less a coward. Not unusually so, but I was never anxious to fight or anything like that. When I got to Vietnam, all of a sudden it was as if I had a death wish. You see, I do a lot of photography, and I'd run toward the action to take pictures. So during my time in Vietnam and Thailand and the Philippines I was living a life of freedom from my previous conception of myself. I covered all battle areas, all PXs. I was the accountant for them all. Even though I went over as a civilian, I did everything the military would do. I never sent anyone into the battle areas alone. For example, my second assignment was in tiger country at the end of the Ho Chi-Minh trail. Of course, I wrote Tina and said, "I think I've made a terrible mistake."

Have I moved a lot? Always. From my very first job. We got married on August 1, 1934, and I was assigned to Washington on June 25, 1935. When it was necessary, we moved. We moved back and forth across the country. I worked in Washington, D.C., four different times. Our children grew up under those circumstances and it didn't seem to hurt them in any way. After I reached the age of fifty-five, after being in thirteen or fourteen government agencies, I had the rare opportunity of early retirement. After twenty-five or thirty or thirty-five years of service—I can't remember which—you could retire with full retirement pay. So I had thirty-five years in at that time and I decided—I discussed it with Tina—I decided to retire.

I was going to teach school; I was going to teach German and Spanish and accounting. I have my teaching certificate and did my student teaching in commercial subjects. I couldn't work for another government agency because that's double-dipping, and you lose a good part of your pension if you do that. One of the men who had worked for me was a retired lieutenant colonel who said, "There's a way around that. If you can get a job in an agency that does not use funds appropriated by Congress—everyone does except for the Army—Air Force Exchange Service, the officers' clubs, and the movie operation that sends films out all over the world to military bases—you can retain your pension. Furthermore," he said, "you might enjoy it." And I did.

So we're going to move from California to Hawaii for this work. It's 1967. I think my sons were not very happy about it because I was going to go away—again. I spent about a third of my married life away from home, you see. So we moved to Hawaii. I don't ever want to leave here. We paid for them to come on visits and they came and weren't particularly happy about it. Until I got sick, I could move anyplace we wanted. We've lived all over the world, except Africa, and I don't know anyplace I'd rather live than here. I don't want to go back to the mainland. We could go back to Long Beach, where we lived for many years, but this is just close enough to our progeny.

We didn't travel very much to see them. They usually came out here. But, as is usual among sons of aging parents, there's only one of them—my oldest son, who was with us during much of our early endeavors—who understands everything about what we did and how we got to where we are. My daughter of course lives here, and my wife speaks to her at least once or twice a week. But the other two boys we've had difficulty with. It's not because they're ignorant. My second boy is the vice-president of a hospital in California. The other is a professor. So, two boys we hardly see and hardly talk to. Does it hurt? Yes. Of course.

[*At this point, Mr. Harding called his wife from another room and asked her to participate in this discussion because, he said, "I want to hear her response."*]

Do they appreciate what we've done and how we've done it? No. I always did things with my children. I was a cub master and a scout master. So it's not that we were disinterested, that we didn't work with them, that we didn't do things together. Maybe if we hadn't been so close to them, we wouldn't have had the problems we have now. But right now, I don't even know if they acknowledge that I'm sick. What have I done wrong?

Tina: I think they can't face Tim's illness. It makes them a little angry. They thought at the beginning that I was doing too much. What was the alternative? [*Tim and Tina say together, as if rehearsed:*] I should come to Long Beach and buy a condominium and raise their adopted son!

The thing that blew our relationship with Donald, our youngest son, was this. We have a house full of old furniture. We can point to any piece and say, for example, "That table we bought in Long Beach thirty years ago." We didn't just go into a store and buy these things. Well, Donald came in with the [his] little boy, a very active little boy. The adopted boy—I won't acknowledge him until he's fifty years old—he started tearing up the house. And I said to my son, who was sitting and looking off into the distance, I said, "He's breaking up the furniture." Donald says, "With a boy his age, you have to expect that he's going to trash the house." I said, "Well, I don't have anything else, and at my age I don't think I'm gonna get it. He can't trash this house." And he said . . . what did he say? The only words I can remember that can be passed down in history are what I said next: "Get off your fat ass and take care of that kid!" Did he? Yeah, he did.

Tina: He'd never heard his father curse before, or anything. It didn't seem like Tim to him, I guess. The youngest one would love for me to be with him. He always felt that, since he was the third boy, a middle child, that he was left out—when in fact he wasn't. Because he and my daughter grew up together. We took them to Europe with us. But the thing that hurts him most is that we never gave him a cent. He had to pay for all his schooling by himself.

Let me tell you about us. Tina was thirteen when we met. We got married before she was seventeen. We decided that we wouldn't have children for at least five years. She was working—from the time she was thirteen she was working like all get out—because I went to St. John's University, plus several other colleges. And St. John's was $8 a semester hour, which now sounds like they were giving it away. But still—where did you get $8 in those hard times?

So she went out when she was fourteen and worked as a bus girl in the Exchange Buffet. Are you familiar with New York? There's a train that runs from downtown New York over to Jersey. The Exchange Buffet is in the area where they sell the tickets. She worked there when she was a little kid, and as she got older she worked in Schrafft's restaurants. I had a government job at the time, but I started at grade 1, which is no longer in existence. That was $1,260 a year, about $25 a week. But I couldn't go to school on that. Without her help, I could never have done my college work.

My wife has a special ability with people. She's warm. People like her, and my sense of humor throws people off. I've been an accountant all my life. I've worked for thirteen, fourteen government agencies. So I know what I'm good at. She knows what she's good at—she's a wonderful seller. She can sell anything to anybody. I have my abilities, so we never had a problem. For instance, in the matter of buying or selling properties, she's come to me with ideas that I immediately pointed out were at least impossible, but she went ahead and did it anyway. In fact, in Long Beach she traded a small piece of property of little value for an apartment house that was four units—two upstairs, two downstairs—and they gave her back a thousand dollars to pay the closing costs. When she told me what she was going to do, I said, "I can prove to you that it's just not possible. I don't think you can do it." But she did it anyway, so in the end we had a lovely apartment house.

The people that we invited to our home were just amazed that we as government personnel were able to get enough money to buy an apartment house. None of them had anything, which was part of being a government employee. So they were just amazed that we were able to have what we had. Nobody thought I should be doing this or she should be doing that. But she's been a tremendous saleswoman since I met her. The people whom we associated with were usually people working for me.

At the time that she sold the apartment house, my director was a GS 15 or GS 16. That was the Air Force Auditor General, but then I converted it into the Department of Defense, the Defense Contract Audit Agency. I took the navy and the army and the air force offices, which were separate, and I set up an office that would take in the three. The regulations were rewritten so that all three services would be performed by one agency. They did the same thing with procurement. They did the same thing with accounting. We reviewed the operations of aircraft plants up and down the West Coast and I became the main terminal auditor. So I consolidated that.

Here's another example: In the early 1940s, when I went to Washington, D.C., you couldn't get a hotel room for more than three days because there were so many people coming in on a temporary basis. One day I sent my wife to the zoo. Right near the zoo is an apartment house on the park that was mostly occupied by congressmen and government executives and so on. I had something to do and she went in and had lunch and, while she was having lunch, the manager of the hotel came by, sat at the table, and talked to the children—I had two at the time—and asked what we were doing there. My wife told him we were having difficulty finding a place to stay. He said, "Listen, I have an apartment that's about five or six rooms. The place is empty. If you like, you can stay there." So I came back from wherever I was and she told me about it and we moved in. And it was marvelous. It was just wonderful. And he charged us what we would have paid for just a room.

Then—I still don't know how the heck she did it—she found out that in Virginia, Falls Church, it was possible to buy a cinder-block house on a large piece of property for about $5,000 or $6,000. And at that time it was just possible to find a place. She told me about it. I said, "Gee, that's wonderful, but how did you manage it?" She said, "I don't really know," but in any event we moved in and lived there for quite a while. And we had the children there with us.

I always allowed Tina to take care of the money and to buy and sell property because she's good at it and I'm not. But lately I have the feeling that she's, not ignoring me, but . . . passing me by. This morning she took the car down to have the antenna fixed. She didn't say anything to me about it that I can remember. She just goes about her business, and I'm not always sure where she is or what she's doing. I have the feeling I'm the late Mr. Harding.

It's difficult for me to judge what's causing what. First I had the brain operation. I have some residual problems from that operation in that periodically . . . periodically means . . . which is the one that means "not every five hours?" The one that means "sporadically?"[1] That's it.—Sporadically. Anyway, maybe once or twice a week my head gets hazy and I have other symptoms. That's the result of the brain operation I had that seven years ago. I also have rheumatoid arthritis; I have pains across my lower back from one hip to the other. My mind has slowed down to a definite extent. I can't do things I used to. For instance, I'm an accountant, but haven't filed my own taxes in three years.

Everything I do has slowed down. I've always been—I was going to say active—I've always been someone who could do things. I did all the electrical work, the carpentry, the gardening, and whatever else that was needed. I've always been able to do that. My daughter has inherited that ability. My daughter is the fixer and maker and so on. I used to put in a screen in a half hour. This time I hired a man, and it's been two days. He still has to paint it and when the wind blows, it blows the shutters shut. I hate that.

I get tired, and when I get tired I lie down. My wife has a different set of requirements. At about six or seven o'clock, after she's made the food and everything, she gets tired because she started her walking earlier, at six or seven in the morning. So she gets tired. At about 6:30 in the evening she'll say, "I'm going to go upstairs, watch my own television, take a bath, and go to sleep." I've been sleeping off and on for a good part of the day and, all of a sudden, I'm wide awake and I watch television and—I don't read much anymore—but I'll watch television. Then at about eleven o'clock she'll call down to see if I'm still here.

I make up her medication. My wife is very strong in many fields, but numbers sometimes confuse her. She takes Cardizem for chest pains; she takes Digoxin for her heart. We have the physician write it on the bottles—what they do, the different pills. Some of them you take two times a day, some of them you take three times a day. It can be confusing. So I have a little plastic case with four enclosures in it and I use three of them. It organizes things. Say, one of them you take in the morning and you don't take it again until evening. The second one you take morning, noon, and evening. I take one that works as a muscle relaxant. I started out taking one tablet before going to sleep. Then the question was, would one tablet be too strong? It might make you sleepy all day. So I'm in the middle of figuring out what to do.

The main difficulty I had with adapting to Parkinson's is that my neurologist is a kook—the technical description is an "asshole." I got that technical description from my son-in-law, the doctor. The neurologist we had told my wife that I had had it, but she didn't tell me until about a year or a year and a half later because she didn't want to cause me distress.

Tina: He told me and I said to him, "Timmy is having enough troubles now because he'd just had that brain tumor operation." And I said, "If we're not sure, let's wait a while and see if it really is that." He said, "I think he has the beginning of Parkinson's." There's nothing you can do about that, so I figured, "Why tell him all those things. He had a million things he was worried about. So I didn't tell him till later on when I felt it was getting worse and he would have to have medication."

I was mad not with him, the kook, but because she didn't tell me. On the other hand, she didn't tell me for a good reason. She didn't want to give me any more problems. So yes, I was very upset that for about a year and a half I went on having all sorts of crazy symptoms, like the tightening of the muscles, the difficulty with speaking, the jerking, the fingers jumping, the crazy way of walking like a little Chinese girl's pitter-patter.[2] Yes, I was upset that she hadn't told me.

So for about a year or two I was having different symptoms without knowing that I had the condition. It was rather difficult for me to adjust to something I didn't even know about. The first problem I had with the Parkinson's was I noticed I had some involuntary movement in two fingers. Lately, I think that a third finger is becoming involved. But these two fingers work independently, and it isn't as though they both go the same way, but one goes one way and the other goes another way as if there was no coordination.

I have so many damn nuisances, and none of them is going to kill me. What has happened is that within the last six months or so—well, until then I didn't have the feeling that I believe is common to a lot of older people, that my life is gone and I might as well commit suicide. I didn't have that feeling at all, but lately I'm starting to check on what drugs are lethal.

I have a problem in that I can't write. I have to print. It's the Parkinson's. Since I did accounting all my life, I'm used to writing very small and very precisely. That's one of the problems that I have. So I started getting little physical problems. I noticed that and, of course—this is kind of a miracle—this ankylosed knuckle. Where you have a joint, if that solidifies, that's the end of movement. Mine solidified. My doctors told me to live with it, and I said no. I got stubborn. I got more information on the subject, and I got a little exercise weight that you strap on. It took me a year and a half, maybe two years. But now, although there's a stiffness there, of course the sheath is invariably tight, I can close my hand. I couldn't before. There was no movement.

I started having difficulty speaking. If I get on the phone and speak to my oldest son—who just called about an hour ago—I suddenly sound as if I'm crying. And this has increased. It isn't as though you have a reaction or you have a movement or a restriction that's permanent. It varies. I don't always have the same reaction. I notice the difficulty in speaking when I get excited. And I started to have that tiptoe way of walking. I noticed myself doing that more. The facial mask—I can't see my face, so I didn't know that I had it.[3] But I started walking with my shoulders bent, which I think is one of the usual symptoms.

I was less and less capable of walking any distance. My wife would say, "Why don't you go for a nice long walk." This would disturb me very much. I can't walk out the back door. My legs don't go where I want them to, the muscles are so tight. Last week I fell twice. Luckily, I was walking with the girl, a home nurse's aide who helps me with the shower. She was holding my arm tightly so when I fell on the steps outside, I didn't hit the ground because she caught me. I taught her how to do that because, when we had our first job in D.C., my companion here [pointing to Tina]—who slips when there's no ice—slipped terribly in the middle of traffic—all of a sudden I'm holding an arm and she's down on the ground! [Both laugh.] So I used to walk with her the way I'm walked with now!

POSTSCRIPT

On one level, Tim and Tina Harding are the stereotypical couple of their generation. He was the successful, self-made businessman who put work before family. Traveling frequently, he was rarely at home and, when there, was a less than demonstrable parent whose "peculiar" sense of humor was probably misunderstood and misread by their children. She was the home-maker, raising a family and supporting her husband whose failings—glaringly evident to their children, apparently—she blindly ignored. And yet, the stereotype is too simple, too pat. He admires her interpersonal skills, her financial abilities, and Tina Harding's demonstrable acumen with real estate. He respects her opinion and asks for it frequently.

His depression and sporadic memory problems (inability to remember words, the "haze" which he says sometimes obscures his world) are almost certainly the result of Parkinson's disease, not the brain tumor excised seven years before this interview. But then, he does have a fair amount to be depressed about. An active man whose life has been physically restricted, he is alienated from the offspring who, he had always presumed, would be support and comfort in infirm age. Further, he faces the certain prospect of declining health—Parkinson's cannot be cured—and perhaps the unspoken fear that his wife may be distanced from him in his extremity.

Mr. Harding emphasizes his work history when asked about his life. This is common among the narrators of this volume. To be fair, however, it is typical of most North American adults. In *Watersheds*, a book about non-senior adult crises, almost every narrator speaks first about his or her work and then, secondarily, about his or her personal life. Simply, we all generally define ourselves in terms of our professional positions. When those have been ended by illness—or forced retirement—then it is the work one did that is first brought forward when people talk about themselves.

With his wife, he is unhappy about his sons' estrangement. Here, however, he focuses on one incident to explain a relationship deeply rooted in the family's life. For a variety of reasons, the Harding children have chosen between their parents, and neither parent wants to accept that Tina is wholly favored over her husband. The simplest explanation for the obvious attachment their children have for Mrs. Harding is that it was she who was always present and whose good humor and warmth—qualities her husband praises—sustained them as they moved from location to location. His parental duties were handled between assignments and, while it is the between time that he most remembers, the children, one suspects, have not forgotten his absences.

This is painful for both Tim and Tina Harding. They don't understand it. Wasn't Tim a scout master? Isn't he proud of his children's achievements, successes enabled by the education and assistance his paycheck provided? Modern children, they look back and remember his many absences, resent his "peculiar sense of humor," and the exacting standards he set. The

Hardings, however, are of a generation in which men like Jake Epps and Tim did what was necessary to feed their family, even when it meant leaving for long periods of time.

NOTES

1. The inability to find a word he knows or a phrase he *almost* remembers may be a residual aftereffect of his earlier brain tumor. Whether related to his Parkinson's or his previous health problems, the sense that the word is there, just beyond his reach, is for most people—and certainly for Mr. Harding—an enormously frustrating, almost humiliating experience.

2. The characteristic "Parkinson's walk," caused by progressive muscular rigidity, has patients on the balls and not the heels of their feet, leaning forward as they walk. Similarly, the involuntary finger movement he next describes—rather like rubbing something between two fingers—is also a common symptom of early Parkinson's disease.

3. The "mask" is usually described as slightly waxen texture with a rigidity of the facial muscles and a generally dour, downturn cast to the face at large.

7

Lloyd's Other Life: The Dancer

Every age develops its own peculiar forms of pathology, which express in exaggerated form its underlying character structure.
Christopher Lasch, *The Culture of Narcissism*, Chapter Two

Elizabeth Greer, seventy-eight, lives in Billsley, Ontario, a small town that has become a suburb of metropolitan Toronto. Her apartment is a ten-minute drive from her son's house, several hours distant from her oldest child's home. It is also a forty-five-minute drive from the home of my neighbors, Jim and Marsha. Marsha is her youngest daughter. I met Mrs. Greer in 1990 and since then we have chatted many times on her periodic visits. When I broached the subject of an interview, Mrs. Greer was amenable and her daughter surprised. "She'll talk your ear off," Marsha warned with fond exasperation. "She loves to complain." I came to the house with my tape recorder on a day when her grandchildren, daughter, and son-in-law were all away. When I entered the house, she was slowly going through a family scrapbook and invited me to join her as the pictures sparked memories.

The Meniere's disease that affects her is a balance disorder that causes sporadic spells of dizziness. Although neither life-threatening nor progressive—it does not lead to other, more serious ailments—its effect on an individual's life, as Mrs. Greer's story illustrates, can be substantial.

S omebody taped my voice before, and I sounded like an old nag. And I was a lot younger then! I love old snapshots. I never took a good picture, but my husband, Lloyd, did. I've got an album for each one of my children, and one for each one of my grandchildren. I look at them every so often, and it brings back good memories. Usually when you're taking snapshots, everybody's happy. Oh, I remember the bad times, too. Like the year that Jackson's Bakery folded, which was hard on Lloyd. He worked there, you know.

I guess all you can hear from me is "my Lloyd." I'm sorry. That's been my life. He was my life. I have happy memories with him. Thank God I have that. I told someone, we never had an awful lot of money, but we always had a lot of laughs. He always had a smile or a joke, and, if I lost my temper, he'd say, "Well! It's time you were backed up against the wall!" [*Laughs*] I've heard so many older people saying, "We've been married for over thirty years, and we've never had a fight." That's a lot of malarkey. I don't believe a couple can be married that many years and not fight, unless they were both deaf. We had some whoppers! And we bickered about money, just like everybody else. Looking back, some of the things we used to fight about were so stupid. I had a bad temper, and he was the type of man you could only push so far. His eyes would flash, but Lloyd was a very forgiving man—more forgiving than me.

He couldn't have stood it to be in a wheelchair, to be a cripple, or to be an invalid. Lloyd loved his garden. He just loved to grow vegetables. He was a workaholic! I think that's what killed him, I really do. My oldest daughter, Judith, says he worked too hard. When he retired he refinished furniture. He refinished that old chair, the one you're sitting in, that belonged to Grandma Greer. And he loved his garden. We had one house. Lloyd built it himself. We bought the lot, and he built it himself. My dad helped him a bit. Lloyd did everything. The only thing he had contracted was the plumbing, the electricity, and the basement. He worked eight, nine hours at Jackson's Bakery, then he'd come home and go out to Billsley. It took ten years off his life, I think. But we loved our home. Yeah, forty-two, forty-three years ago now. It was Judith's birthday when we moved in. She was a year old.

I thought I would go long before Lloyd. I've had a lot of sickness in my life. Different things happened to me that seemed worse than they were. Not serious things, but for a whole year I was ill with a very bad cough. This was when the children were little. I was in the hospital for six weeks. They did a bronchoscopy, and then they put me on that awful pill, Prednisone,[1] which I think is terrible. They said that I had emphysema. But then much later, after I went back to work—and I was nervous after not working for thirty-five, thirty-six years—I started to get this shortness of breath. So the doctor made an appointment for me with this specialist up at St. Joseph's. Then when I went back to see him a second time, he asked, "Who told you that you have emphysema?" I said, "Well, it doesn't matter anyway because he's dead now." So the doctor said, "Well, he was wrong. If you had emphysema, your lungs would be marked. And they're not. I think it was nerves, and I think that's what's wrong with you now."

Lloyd never had any sickness, and then he had a hernia, which he had operated on two years before the heart attack. It's five years in August. Lloyd died very suddenly. He wouldn't go see the doctor. This is how it happened. We always liked to lay in the mornings. We'd been to Expo '86 in Vancouver, and he'd complained of indigestion on the drive there. Well, on the drive back the same thing happened. And I said to him, "I want you to go see our doctor when we get home." He said, "Oh, it's just indigestion." Well, he looked fine. I'll never forget the date or the time—it was a quarter to eight—and I said, "Oh, I can't lay around any longer, Lloyd," and I went to get out of bed. That was when I heard this sort of . . . he put his hand out, and I turned around. His face was all blank—just like that. But there was no sign of anything.

He was just stubborn. Most of it was his own fault. He just would not go to see the doctor. The doctor told me, "You know, if you could have talked him into coming to see me about all these indigestion attacks he was having, we could have saved him." The day after I buried him, I picked up his picture and gave him hell. You get all the bitterness out of the soul after a while. There were too many good things about him to stay mad. I remember my friend, Allan, and he said when Lloyd died, "I never said anything to you, but Lloyd was like a second dad to me."

My children were my mainstay when Lloyd died, even though they weren't near me. They loved their father dearly. I came to visit Marsha in Toronto, and I was down in the States with Judith—they kept me for two or three weeks. But when you get to be older and you're alone and go to visit—even when you love your children dearly—you want to get home. You know, to your own bed, your own surroundings. People in my church were just unbelievable, just wonderful. Lloyd was an elder at the church, very well loved. He used to do a lot of things for them at the church, when things would go wrong. He'd help the other men. He couldn't do it when he was working, because he worked Saturdays. So when he retired, he wanted to give as much as he could. He wasn't what you'd call a real religious man, but he enjoyed the men at the church. Everybody loved him in the neighborhood. He had one of the largest funerals that I've seen in Billsley for a man who actually wasn't in the public eye all the time. I thought the cards would never stop. It's as if it happened yesterday.

How we met, well . . . my aunt had a boardinghouse on James Street South in Windsor. There were a lot of boardinghouses up there. They'd been beautiful homes at one time, belonging to wealthy people. My aunt was a wee, tiny person. I went up there to stay with her for awhile. I was a skinny thing, with my hair cut in a Buster Brown. I had horn-rimmed glasses and weighed about thirty-five pounds. I came home one night—I'd been out with a boy my aunt didn't like—and Lloyd was sitting in the kitchen with her, talking. And she said, "Lloyd, I'd like you to meet my niece." And then she says, "Elizabeth likes to dance, Lloyd."

She had this Irish accent. She was as Irish as Patty's pig. And her name was Sarah Malone; she was the second cousin to my mother, and she managed that boardinghouse—it was four stories—she managed it with an iron fist. Boy, nobody tried anything on Aunt Sarah. And I said, "You don't have to ask me out." I was embarrassed! And he said, "No, I'd like to take you dancing." He had wicked eyes! And I said, "Well, I don't know if I want to go out with you." He was very much the gentleman. We went to the Conners Hotel, he took me there, and he said, "Would you like to go downstairs for a drink?" And I said I didn't drink. So he said, "I know where I'm going to take you then." And he took me into the drugstore that was in the Conners Hotel and bought me a soda. I was twenty-two. And that was it, yeah. He had beautiful teeth. Wicked eyes and beautiful teeth. [*Laughs.*]

We weren't going to get married. We were one of these couples who said, "When the war is over." But at that time we couldn't have gotten married anyway. His father had been very ill out west, and they had told him that he should never work again. He was a blacksmith and the work was too heavy. So Lloyd came east and got this job and sent home for his parents. He got an apartment for them. It was only about a year later that we met and wanted to get married but couldn't because of looking after his parents. Then when the war broke out, his father got a job because they were looking for older men. It wasn't a hard job. So then Lloyd got into the service. And I was in the service too, one of those "Canadian women serving in the armed forces." WACs, we were called. I got as far as Kitchener and they found out I was office material, and that was it. That's where I stayed. I did have basic training, but that came about a year after I was in the force.

I met this one girl in the service. She was so beautiful; she was married to this lieutenant. We got pregnant about the same time. She bunked in with me and she used to tell me all about her husband who was coming home on leave. And her father was a commander over in England. She couldn't get into her uniform and they weren't discharging her. I was being discharged because of my mother—she was very ill and needed someone to look after her. I got home, and when Lloyd found out I'd been discharged, he came home, and we were married in June. Then I went out west with him.

Then he went overseas. When he came back, it was just beautiful. I mean, the reunion was great—all our parents were there and everybody—and we stayed with his mum and dad for a few months. Then his mum and dad were selling the big house they were in, and Lloyd got them a little cottage. We had to live with my parents for a few months. Then a friend of Lloyd's at Jackson's Bakery came in one morning and said, "Elizabeth, I think I have an apartment for you." He said, "Get yourself dressed and go over and take a look." And I said, "I've got to take Judith. I don't think they'll take me if I have a little girl, but they have to know." So I got her all spiffed up and went over—and I got the apartment. I was just in shock. And when Lloyd came home I said, "We've got an apartment!" It was like seventh heaven. There was a little tiny hall on the second floor of the house, and the bathroom was almost as big as the living room. And then a small bedroom and a little, eat-in kitchen. It was like a palace. We just couldn't believe it. We were so happy there.

I was a spoiled child. My parents had a lot of money when I was little. Lost everything in the Depression. My Dad lost both stores. He was quite well off and then lost everything. I got a little independent, working and all that. My first job I worked was at the soda fountain when I was still going to school. I hated that. I didn't like the way boys treated you. After that, I didn't work for about a year. Then I quit school and got a job in a candy factory. Swore I'd never eat a chocolate in my life after that. And then I finally got a job in advertising. I drew chickens for this [advertising] campaign and helped the lady who answered the French correspondence—all her letters—because I knew a bit of French. I worked there for four years. Earned $8 a week. And it cost us seven cents on the streetcar every day for me to get to work!

When I got married to Lloyd, he spoiled me. He did everything. He looked after the books—I had a budget that I looked after—and that was why it was so very difficult for Lloyd when Jackson's folded. It was very hard on his ego. He had been a man who looked after his family. I was at home; I was a homemaker. He got a job working at a hardware store, and he hated being inside, my Lloyd. When Jackson's Bakery sold out, he was fifty-one. I remember I typed up résumés, and we mailed them out. The same letters would come back. He was fifty-one years old and nobody wanted him. They didn't *say* that, but you could read between the lines. He was sales manager at Jackson's. Then he was nothing.

So after Jackson's closed, I started working again. Women working? Lloyd didn't like it. But there was nothing he could do. Had to. The year that Jackson's folded, Judith was getting married in July, Marsha was going into university in September, and Paul was going into high school. Still, we had to cancel half the marriage we had planned. It was the children who came to us and said, "There's no way you can afford a big, fancy marriage." So we went to our church and ordered everything right from the church. The women's club took it over, and it was just wonderful.

Anyway, I taught Sunday school for, I guess, twenty years. And I loved that. After Jackson's folded, I typed for the church, and then I started to do the memos for the superintendent of the local school at the school board. It was real nice working for them. I loved it. I loved the children. I still meet them up on King Street. "How are you, Mrs. Greer!" "How are you? What are you doing?" And I've been retired ten years at this time! I helped them with their graduation at the school—I made all the graduation diplomas by hand.

The sad part was, you got to know the ones who got into trouble when you worked in the office. I can tell you about two cases. One was a little boy who was in our special education class. The teacher had an awful time with him, so she'd bring him up to me. And I'd get crayons out for him. But his main joy was being able to sit behind me and watch me type. When he took a bad turn, he'd go right into a fetal position. It was very sad. He was the result of two parents, one with ten children and one with eleven. And he is now in a special care unit. I heard that he died. His name was Paul, same as my son. We had a little girl drown when I was at the school. And it was sad. You see a lot of carelessness, and that used to hurt me. I never saw any battered children, but some were coming to school with potato chips and pop for lunch instead of a thermos of soup and some milk. And our nurse, when I first went there, she used to tell me stories about the food these children would bring to school. And it was terrible.

We used to go dancing about twice a month, down to the Boat Club. Lloyd just loved to dance. We were down there one night and saw Bobby Feldon, and found out he was married to my mother and father's best friend's daughter, which I didn't know. He grew up with me in the north end of Hamilton. Anyway, Bobby Feldon was the sales manager for a while at the local dairy, so he came over to the table, sat down, and asked Lloyd, "Well, how're you making out?" And he said, "Well, I just hate the job I'm doing." So Bobby said, "Well, I'm going to give your name to the boss, Mr. Hummel." And Lloyd went down and got the job. Same job as he did at Jackson's, delivering. And he loved that, but like everything else, he was a lot smarter than many other people. He had a university education. But during the Depression you couldn't get a job if you were a Bachelor of Science. So after they found this out at the dairy, they moved him into the office. But he didn't like the job as much.

MENIERE'S DISEASE

The first time it struck me, I was on the street and they rushed me to the hospital. Some people get it lighter than others. I got it very, very bad. I've been in hospital twice with this stupid Meniere's because I fall down. I went to the specialist and he told me, "Well, I sorta' figured you'd be having Meniere's disease from the way your ear was going." I'm completely deaf on one side, but there's good hearing in the other ear. And the doctor asked me, "Do you drive? I'm afraid you're going to have to phone your insurance company, because I don't think they'll cover you." So I called them and they said, "You're very honest. But no, we couldn't possibly cover you. And if you had an accident, we wouldn't be able to pay for anything."

I never took the car uptown to the city after Lloyd died. And I never went outside of Billsley. I was a nervous driver, but I think I was a good driver. I only had one accident in my whole life, in thirty-five years of driving. I guess I was too careful. Maybe a lot of people didn't like being behind me. Marsha is so calm driving in Toronto—and I'm so nervous—but if someone got mad at me, I lost my temper. I'm awful that way.

For example, they'd put a new light in on the road, and I didn't know you could make a left-hand turn at the stoplight if there wasn't any traffic. So I waited. There was this great big tractor trailer behind me. He put his hand on the horn and I must have jumped five feet. Then he zoomed right by me. I followed him until he stopped. Then I got out of the car, and he got out and said, "What's the matter, Ma'am?" And I said, "Don't you ever do that to me again! Don't you ever blow your horn again. You scared the bejeebers out of me." And I said, "I couldn't turn. That was a left-hand turn." He was standing there and I know he must have been trying to keep from laughing, because he must have been six foot four and he must have weighed over 200 pounds. And here I am hoppin' like a hen. And he was very nice and he apologized. Very soft spoken. But he said, "I think you should know you can make a left-hand turn there if there's no traffic." When I told the kids, Paul said, "Mother! You could have had a real bad one." The children told me, "You don't know who you're talking to—you should be careful."

Not driving, I lost my independence. That's the hardest thing. I don't go to the seniors' group anymore since I don't have a car. I stopped going to auction sales in beautiful little towns. I have a very dear friend in Woodstock who is dying of leukemia and I have to depend on another friend to drive me every time I want to go see her. It is harder. Visiting the kids is harder. I'd have to get a bus on King Street in Billsley, then you take a transfer to the King West bus in Windsor, then you get the bus at the terminal in Toronto, and you're luggin' luggage all the while. It's much tougher than being able to tuck your luggage into your car, turn your key, and away you go.

It's independence more than anything. Just this spring, things that I need—like things for your balcony, for flowers—you've got to ask people to drive you to pick these things up, because you can't do it on the bus. People are very good, don't get me wrong. You have no idea how really nice people can be. I just don't like calling people to drive me. Before, I helped a lot of my friends who didn't drive; I used to take them different places in the car. I used to help drive other people around, friends—not as a volunteer. Just to help people, you know? I have volunteered in the past. We have a new hospital and I have my name down as a volunteer in there.

This euchre club that Lloyd and I belonged to, they didn't want me to quit when Lloyd died. Vera and Maurice and Lloyd and I started the club forty years ago. These are friends that we have been with for so many years. Then, when your husband dies, people try their best to keep in touch, maybe by phone. They want to include you in things, but it's not the same thing. I did go back, and I did play cards for two years. Then when I got this Meniere's, I figured it wouldn't be fair. We have six couples and we take turns having all twelve people for dinner. That takes six of the winter months. It makes things go fast. Well, I couldn't look after twelve people with this, because I never knew when I'd get it, when it would hit me. It would usually hit me when I was upset, and if I had to get a meal for twelve people without Lloyd, it would be upsetting. So I've lost that camaraderie that I had before.

Well, I was a good fifteen minutes' walk to the stores, and I couldn't have walked to my doctors in the winter time. Cabs are expensive, so I sold my car and put the house up for sale. It wasn't a big house; it's a one-and-a-half with a dormer on the side. We had three bedrooms upstairs, living room, dining room, kitchen. A nice rec. room in the basement that Lloyd built himself—lot of good memories. He built our cupboards there himself. And

Paul was born there, in that house. It had a lot of memories. I don't go back very often. This new man who bought it has cut all the trees down. I think Lloyd would turn over in his grave.

It was really hard on Marsha—the move. I caught her crying in the car one day when I was getting things moved and that. For me, without Lloyd, it wasn't the same. I'll be quite honest with you, I'd had an offer on the house the year after Lloyd passed away, but that was when Marsha's first husband left and she didn't have someone to turn to. I had this young real-estate agent, and I said to him, "I'm not going to sell it now. I'm sorry. My daughter needs a haven to come home to." So I stayed there for four years after Lloyd died. That's when I got the dog. And the children always came home.

When I did move, I had to find a good home for my little dog because they were not allowed in the apartment building. But I miss him, my poodle. They are very, very understanding dogs. He'd be laying beside me on the couch. I'd be listening to some old records and I'd start crying. He'd put his two little paws on my shoulders and start licking my face. We don't give animals a lot of credit for brains, but they sometimes are more kind than we are. He wasn't the same as my first one. Isn't it funny? Georgie, my first, had papers. A pedigree. So did Sandie, but he was a different type of dog. Very very hyper. I guess the neighbors all thought I was crazy to keep him because he had me running after him half the time. Of course, after Lloyd died, the whole neighborhood treated me like Grandma. You know, because I was alone, they were all very concerned, and they didn't like to see me chasing around after him.

Did you know how I got him? Georgie was killed by the pit bulls. Joel Hurley at the local radio station had a little apricot poodle just like mine, so they called from the station and asked if he could interview me when he heard about Georgie being killed. I didn't want to be interviewed on the radio. I don't like publicity. But he wanted to know if I would accept another little dog. And because they were so kind, I said I would take it. But I really didn't want to. It was too soon. And he found that out too. When I was giving little Saddie away, the second poodle, I called his secretary to see if he would take little Saddie back. And his apricot poodle had died. And he said no, it was too soon.

Now, I'm not really looking toward anything. I guess I'm like this ninety-year-old lady that I met out at the seniors' club. She was the brightest old thing and I said, "I hope I'm as bright as you are if I have to live to be ninety." And she said, "Well, if you get to be my age, when you wake up in the morning, you say, 'Thank you, God, for another day.' " And this is the way I go. I don't have any dreams about any future, because I sure don't want to meet anybody. I'd make another man miserable anyway. [*Laughs.*]

I don't like to think of being in a hospital and being in a wheelchair. Tied to a wheelchair. I've seen too much of that. There was my mother and Lloyd's mother. Mother wasn't too bad, because she still had all her wits about her. She had an aneurysm; that's what killed my mother in the end. But Grandma Greer, she was ninety years old. She was as smart as a pin. And then she just went downhill so fast, it was terrible. And we used to go to visit her, and they'd all be sitting in wheelchairs, all tied in. That is the one thing if I think about it—well, I try not to think about it.

These are lonely years. Very lonely. I have friends who go out to play cribbage, they go to whist, they go to shuffleboard, billiards. These are all things I'm not interested in. And I'm not interested in going to the dances that they try and get me to go to. I did go to aerobics. It's great, and I enjoyed that, but I don't go to that anymore because of the Meniere's. My legs are good—I don't know what they look like—but they're good to walk on. I like to walk. I go for a walk nearly every morning, as long as it's not raining or snowing too hard. I loved to cycle, but I went and sold my bike. Now I wish I had it back. But when streets get pretty busy it's sort of hard to ride a bicycle when you get to be my age. You get a little bit dottery, you know? I have the women's group at our church. I go once a month, but you have thirty days in between.

I talk to the walls in the apartment now. Apartment living isn't the same. In a house you've got freedom. You can go out in the garden. You can go out your side door, your front door, your back door. In an apartment you've got a balcony and that's about it. I've got a nice apartment, I've got things a lot better than a lot of women my age. Believe you me, I'm very grateful for what I have. Folks talk to you on the elevator, but most people my age have their own friends. And they get sorta' settled. My other friend lives up in St. Agnes Retirement Village up in Windsor. Beautiful little cottages.

I think my friend was a little disappointed that I didn't move up there, but my children weren't too happy about the idea. And my church, the people from my church who were so good when Lloyd died—and all my neighbors and everything were here—my seniors' group and my friends. Everything was right here in Billsley. You can get here in five minutes from where my son lives. But one thing about St. Agnes Village: you've got people and you can have an animal. You can have a little dog. And there's a swimming pool about five minutes from where the cottages are. But I'd still be leaving all my friends. That was my choice, and the fact that I wouldn't be leaving anything to the kids if I bought one of those cottages. Now I'm at least leaving something.

If the children were closer, it wouldn't be so bad. I was here in Toronto at Christmas, Easter, and now in July. And I'll be here in the fall. I don't get to see Judith too often, with them living in Oneida, New York. Judith married very well-to-do. Her husband, Paul, teaches at a university near there. He's a bit of a male chauvinist, but she's made a go of her marriage. I go there about once a year. Her boys are into sports now. They're busy. You know, they have to live their own lives now. Busy. They have their own lives to live, and it's hard enough today for young couples to stay together without having somebody they're worried about all the time. This is my independence—this I like. I try to tell them not to worry about me. I'm on the ALERT system.[2] It's great. If anything goes wrong at home, I first call ALERT.

I see Paul most every week. I can take the bus up to Paul's; it only costs me a dollar. He's my baby. He's just like his dad. He's not as good at helping around the house as his dad was. Lloyd could bake better than I did. He made a better pie than I did. Paul is to be thirty-nine this November. Paul has a wonderful marriage. She's a good girl and a wonderful homemaker. She made all my drapes and beautiful cushions for my bed. But instead of calling me "Mother," she calls me "Grandma." Four children. He had the three little girls, and now this little boy. He said to me, "Mother, he's the best 'mistake' I ever made."

Would I think of living with any of my kids? No, absolutely not. It's just not fair to them. It's not fair to have an older person in the house. Two women in a kitchen, for one thing, isn't very good. My mother lived with me for sixteen years before she went out on her own. They built a seniors' apartment in Hamilton, and she wanted to go there. I felt she needed it, and we needed it too. It's not the same for a young couple to have an older person in the home with you. If Lloyd and I had an argument, my mother would go upstairs. Afterward, she wouldn't come downstairs and say, "Now I know, dear, he shouldn't have done this." She never took sides. Never. She and Lloyd got along so great.

She was a wonderful woman. My mother and father were a case where they shouldn't have stayed together, but she stayed with my father because of us. Things just went downhill, but she stayed with him. He finally left her and she stayed with us. When my father was dying, I drove up about every other day I could. And when he was dying, he asked for her. So I called the house, and I said, "Could you bring Grandma up here?" And my mother sat and held his hand until he passed away. When she died, she could have been buried up in a beautiful part of the cemetery with her mother and father, but she was buried with him. All he had to do was lift his little finger, and she would have gone to him. I couldn't have done what she did. I'd have killed him.

I know of people whose children have built an apartment in their house and the parents live there. That would be okay. But right now it's too expensive to do that. Paul wanted to build an apartment for me in the basement of his house, but he had this band. And I said, "I couldn't live down there when you were practicing. Drive me crazy." I put up with it for ten years before he got married. I've got my independence as far as staying in my apartment, but it's lonely. You could go playing cards every day and go out dancing every Saturday night and go to church every Sunday. And meet everybody that you knew and go out to supper. But you'd still come home to an apartment where there's nobody, not even a little dog to talk to. That is the hardest part of being old, I think. I really do.

POSTSCRIPT

Several months after this interview Mrs. Greer moved from the apartment she had inhabited to the seniors' community she was considering in her narrative. The decision was courageous, requiring a substantial financial investment made over the reservations of her children. It meant using capital that she thought of as "legacy," a future bequest for her children, for immediate needs. Moving also required an emotional shift from her community of history—the town she had shared with her husband—to one that reflected her contemporary need and status. It thus embraced both a break with the past and an emphasis on her own present need over the potential of a future legacy for her adult children.

The decision was as therapeutic as it was practical. In the years since that move she has been much, much happier than she was on the day of the interview. Besides the friend who preceeded her, she has made new friends in this senior's setting, people with whom she shares activities and interests. Since her new community not only permits but encourages its members to have pets, Mrs. Greer has a new companion. Her dog, Hammett, is a constant object of her concern. When she visits her children, Hammett travels with her. On their visits I see him waiting, impatiently, for her to take him on his morning walk. "I talk to him all the time," she explained, "and he listens."

There comes a time when children of the elderly treat their seniors with a certain fond exasperation, when the roles of parent and offspring no longer wear easily for either party. Certainly the Greers—mother and daughter—were at this point when I interviewed Elizabeth. In an attempt to be both busy and "useful" each visit, Mrs. Greer would clean her daughter's refrigerator, rearrange and clean the kitchen shelves, and cook meals her grandchildren ate but did not necessarily relish. Her daughter, Marsha, accepted these intrusions with good humor and fond exasperation. "She needs to do *something*," she said to me. "But after all, it is all my house."

These minor frictions aside, the relations between Mrs. Greer and her children remain close. She occasionally "baby sits" her teenage children, for example, when both Marsha and her husband are out of town. Clearly, however, it is to her son, "my baby," that she turns most frequently. He is geographically the closest and, emotionally, perhaps, the one most intimately related to his mother. But Mrs. Greer's concern about her second oldest daughter—evidenced by her refusal to sell a house she had emotionally and physically outgrown because the then recently divorced Marsha needed its continuity in *her* life—is clear. Soon after the interview took place, Marsha married the man with whom she had been living for several years, one committed both to her and to her children. Mrs. Greer's relieved comment was, "Good! Now I can die in peace." Her daughter, Marsha, repeated this anecdote with fond exasperation, adding with a laugh, "Typical of these old folks, isn't it?"

Perhaps. Clearly, caring does not cease with age. Certainly, feelings of responsibility for children and friends continue for a lifetime. Equally common is the discomfort adult children feel in the presence of an elderly parent's ongoing sense of responsibility for and to an adult child.[3] But as this and other narratives make clear, Mrs. Greer matured in a culture where responsibility for others was a definition of adulthood. Her husband cared for his parents, providing them with a cottage before building a home for his immediate family; she resigned from the military to care for her mother, who lived with her for sixteen years "before she went out on her own."

Like Sherry Busch and Holly Treeson, Mrs. Greer was indoctrinated from an early age in the ethos of caring for others, especially those who are older and more fragile. At the same time, she and the others in this book insist on independence as a primary virtue. Mrs. Greer is adamant that living in the home of any of her children would be an imposition that necessarily would diminish her life and sense of self-esteem. And yet, her mother was easily integrated into her home and relations with her husband's parents, for whom he cared, were excellent. I asked her about this apparent inconsistency and she shrugged. "Those were different times," she said.

Perhaps that difference lies in this: the balance between caring and independence once common to many women has been replaced by an emphasis on independence as the primary virtue. Those who cared for others—professionally or in a familial context—found independence in that role. To be the receptor of another's care, however, is to be dependent and thus a failure. The duality of caregiver and receiver no longer carries equal weight.

It is common these days to sneer at the subordinate role accepted by women of this generation. These narratives offer an interesting critique of these modern assumptions. Independence and self-reliance were as important to these women as they were to their partners. But it was, for them, a virtue that simultaneously existed *with* caring. That they themselves might become dependent was something these women never considered.

It was women like Sarah Malone who once presented the ideal mixture of independence and solicitude. Aunt Sarah was warm and caring, smart and tough. "She managed it [the boardinghouse] just with an iron fist," Mrs. Greer recalls fondly. "Boy, nobody tried anything on Aunt Sarah." It was Aunt Sarah who showed how, amid the traditional duties of cooking and cleaning—household tasks—independence could be established. Clearly, it is a lesson Elizabeth Greer learned. Although her life was defined by her husband and their relation ("All you'll hear from me is my Lloyd"), she was never "merely" a wife or a pliant helpmate to a domineering male. When they needed money, she went back to work despite his objections. The job she found provided independence in a post that allowed her to care for other, younger people who needed her. Indeed, in this she followed precisely in her aunt's footsteps.

In their marriage she was never a silent partner. Elizabeth Greer remembers with relish the battles she and Lloyd fought; delights in telling about how they would argue. In missing the companionship of her life's mate, she mourns the loss of a sparring partner who would fight with her, argue with her as an equal. Characteristically, perhaps, she was so angry at his death that she lectured Lloyd's photograph after his death.

And so today she battles for her own place while seeking someone who needs her. She will happily care for another—indeed, she seeks responsibility—while rejecting wherever possible being the object of care herself. Thus, while she happily chauffeured friends of hers for years she is today loathe to ask others for a ride. Clearly, she would deny the generally accepted, scholarly assumption that seniors are owed a primordial debt by their children, or that because they assisted their seniors they must, in their turn, be maintained by this generation of adult children.

NOTES

1. Prednisone is a frequently prescribed steroid of enormous use in a number of conditions. It was "terrible" for Mrs. Greer because of side effects she apparently suffered.

2. This is a "buddy" system in which seniors call each other if a problem occurs. Each is charged with the care of another, and each calls the other every day to assure that he or she is all right. There is also a mechanical "alert," a device worn around the neck that can ring a central exchange. Thus, for example, if one falls and is unable to get up or get help, by pushing the button, help can be reached automatically.

3. See, for example, Tom Koch, *Mirrored Lives: Aging Children and Elderly Parents* (Westport, CT: Praeger, 1990).

8

Lodgings

Let the athletes die young and laurel-crowned.
Let the soldiers earn the Purple Hearts.
Let women die old, white-crowned, with human hearts.
　　Ursula K. Le Guin, "The Space Crone," in *Dancing at the
Edge of the World: Thoughts on Words, Women, Places, 1997

My friend, Vancouver physician Bill McArthur, thought I should meet a person who was not merely "old," but what social gerontologists call "old-old."
And so he introduced me to Heather Grissom. Certainly, she qualifies. A
member of the extreme set of age, those who continue past ninety years,
when Heather Grissom speaks of "The War," she's talking about World War
I, not its successor. At the time of our interview she lived with her daughter,
Anne, her best friend, and, to the extent she needed it, her caregiver. Both
were present when we talked. When the older woman paused in her narrative, searching for a date, perhaps, it is her daughter who provided it, and
sometimes a minor commentary on the life they've together known.

I didn't learn to cook as a girl in Aberdeen. Mother always said she
couldn't afford to let me learn in case I spoiled whatever I was trying
to make. It would be too expensive. So I never learned to cook. All I
did was look after the children. I was one of a big family, one of the older
ones, and I was always the nursemaid. My mother would always prefer to
do work than look after the children, so I looked after them in our house.

And when I left home for Edinburgh, I went to look after another couple's child.

Then, when I was about eighteen or nineteen—when I had been working as a nursemaid in Edinburgh—my mother had another baby. And she wrote and asked if I would go home for a while to Aberdeen. So I went home for about a year, and while I was there I met an Anglican minister and his wife who lived quite close to us. She asked me if I had done children's nursing and I said, yes, that was all I had ever done. So she asked me how I would like to come out to Canada with a family, bring their baby out, and care for him. I said I didn't know, I'd have to think about it. I did, and decided that maybe I should make the change. So I came out with this husband and wife and their three-month-old baby that I looked after because it was their first baby and she didn't know much about it at all. I looked after him until he was about eighteen months old.

That was during wartime, 1914. We were going to come out in August and they postponed our sailing until September. We were in darkness all the way out. No lights at night, you know, for safety. We went over around when the *Lusitania* went down and I think another ship had gone down, too. Torpedoed. And I came out to Regina with them for a year and a half.

Then I went nursing another family. After that, the Robert Simpson Company came out from Toronto and opened a branch in Regina, so I got a chance to work there. I was there for quite a while. They had a summer resort at a lake and a manager asked me if I'd like to go down there and work for the summer. So, of course, I thought that was another opportunity. That was in 1917, and his wife had just had a baby and it was my vocation to look after babies. It was common, then. New mothers didn't know much about looking after children in those days. Always looking after babies—that was what I knew.

At the resort I also learned to wait tables. I didn't like it too much. I was scared, trying to remember all those dishes. The work wasn't very easy. I met my husband there. He and his brother ran this summer resort. He looked after the livery and the boats. He drove a car, and in those days people didn't have cars like they do today. They were few and far between. So he had to go to the train station at all different hours to pick up passengers to come to the hotel for two weeks' holiday, or whatever time they had. And then he had the boats as a sideline. He had seven or eight rowboats for rent and he looked after the renting, the painting, and the keeping them in shape.

And so we lived there for a time. My daughter Anne was born there, and my other daughter, too. We had the two girls: Anne and her sister. Then my husband decided he wanted to come out to Vancouver. And so we came out here [Vancouver] and tried to run a fish and chip café. We went broke, of course. It was during the 1930s. The dirty '30s—1934 I think it was. And so we went back that summer to run another resort at Saskatchewan Beach. And it was another failure. People didn't have the money to spend on a resort in those days. Everybody was hard up.

Then my husband's brother was made manager of the Kitchner Hotel in Regina, and my husband worked for them for two years. He then ran a country hotel for seven or eight years, and then we came out to Vancouver again in 1943. We've been here ever since. He bought a house on McDonald Street. It was a big place and it had two, maybe three rentals. A revenue house. In rooming houses you have a lot of work, keeping the place clean and such. We didn't know there were restrictions on where you could have a rooming house, however. And so, of course, the people nearby took up a petition to get us out of there. They didn't want us to have a rooming house. We were there for about two years, I guess, before my husband resold it.

Meanwhile, he had a nervous breakdown. So we went to Ocean Park for a year to a cottage we rented out there. While we were there his sister and her husband came out from Saskatoon to rent a cottage, too. They also were hotel people. And then, one day walking on a beach, he took a heart attack. His wife wouldn't live in the place they had rented so they came to stay with us for a year. Then my brother-in-law bought a house in Vancouver.

So we joined forces. I looked after the house that my brother-in-law bought. We lived there, but didn't pay anything, just helped with expenses. And my sister-in-law helped looking after her mother at that time. Her mother was in a nursing home in Vancouver, so my sister-in-law was going down there every day, looking after them.

One day, my husband was visiting the mother and he happened to see a house on Beach Avenue that was a rooming house, pretty much run down, and he thought it was just the ideal place because it was right on the waterfront and that was where he wanted to be. We bought it, and gradually got it into some kind of shape. We were there for about eight years.

Then, we were invited to visit some friends for Boxing Day dinner. And as we came to Burrard Bridge, driving over, he saw it. Coming home about ten o'clock, my husband said, "There's a fire someplace." Then, as we came off the bridge, he saw it. "That's our house," he said. And it was. It was just gutted. It was a mess. We didn't have a home anymore. So we had to start again.

Meanwhile, my husband had taken cancer of the throat and he was suffering from that. We stayed with friends for about a week while Anne and her uncle looked for some place for us to live. They found us a suite on York Street, where we lived for about a year. My husband was still looking for a place where we could make a living during that time. Then he found a place around Fourteenth and Hemlock we could buy and rent rooms. We spent seven or eight years before we sold it for a fairly good profit.

By then, my husband was quite sick. He kept going and having treatments. At this time, Anne and I found this place on Sixteenth Avenue just near the railroad tracks. It had a nice living room, nice kitchen, and two bedrooms. We lived there and rented the rest of the house. We had a VON [Victoria Order of Nursing] nurse come in and give my husband an injection every night. Except for then, and when he was in hospital, we looked after him. And it was so hard because he couldn't eat.

To see someone in a shape like that, you really feel like it's a blessing when they go because they suffer so much. He reached a point where he couldn't eat. And that's when Dr. Williams, our doctor for years, said, "He won't die of cancer. He'll die of hunger." And that was right. I don't think it's right to keep people when they're not going to get better and life doesn't mean much to them. Then it's more painful than passing on.

My husband died in 1966. Anne and I stayed in that place about a year after my husband died before we went into a rental suite down on Eighth Avenue. Then we saw, a year later, the advertisement for this apartment we're in now. It said "big rooms" and we'd been used to that. So we came here, and we've been here ever since. Twenty-three years.

After my husband died, about six years running Anne and I traveled. I couldn't go anywhere when he was sick. But we made up for it when he was gone. We went to Hawaii. We went to Germany and Italy. In Rome, we even saw the Pope. He was installing a cardinal! In 1970, we visited my family in Scotland. I used to talk about "home" and my husband would say, "This is your home. Not there." But most of my family is there, except my two brothers in New Zealand. And they were just babies when I left. When we visited in 1970 one of my sisters put on a dinner party for us and all the relatives around the area. There must have been twenty people!

I was back once before that. While we were on Beach Avenue, in 1954, I was back to see my parents for two or three weeks. That was my first visit in forty years. My mother and dad were still living at that time, but my mother had a heart condition. I just got back about a month when she died. I was so glad I'd gone back to see them before that. For years, my dad was just a farm worker and then they bought a farm of their own. And, of course, they had enough family to help them run it. I had five brothers. We all stayed in touch by letter. All the time.

We've done not too bad. I think I've had a wonderful life. I've never had any really serious health problems before just last year. Well, in 1949, I had a cerebral hemorrhage. I lay on my back for six weeks and all they fed me was Jell-O! But I got over this and apparently it didn't leave any bad effects, which is amazing. Most people when they have a cerebral hemorrhage it affects their memory or their health quite strongly. But I recovered completely.

A few years ago I couldn't believe I was nearing one hundred years. I never thought about getting old. We had all the childhood disease, like measles, and scarlet fever and chicken pox. We went through it all. This last year, however, I haven't been too well. I had this kidney infection, and then I had the bowel trouble [diverticulitis]. I've really not gotten over it. I'm ready now, anytime, to pass along.

Just the other day I got the step-in walker. Dr. McArthur brought it because he thought I might fall without it and break a hip. As far as the cane is concerned, Anne and my other daughter bought it for me when I was ninety or ninety-five. I've had it quite a few years. Anne takes me out. Just yesterday, we went out to Lulu Island to get some strawberries.

Dr. McArthur comes once a month; he always comes to see me. He's been wonderful. We had a doctor for years, Dr. Williams, who looked after my husband and the rest of the family. And then when he reached the age of sixty-five or sixty-six he had to retire. He couldn't practice surgery any more and that's what he liked. He sold his practice to a doctor named White who we saw for a year, two years or so. But every time I'd go to see him there'd be a different doctor there. You never knew who would be there to see you. Then I met Dr. McArthur and we decided he was the man for us. It's him we see each time, not a lot of strangers. He knows us. And because I don't get out much, he comes here to see me.

My family has been just wonderful to me. Most families are not. I had some friends where the dad died and the girls had to look after the mother. And they'd kind of push her around, and, well, they just weren't very nice. It's not very easy looking after someone who has something wrong with them. My daughters have looked after me, however. And Anne, she's never complained. The other daughter lives up in the Okanagan [in the B.C. interior] and she comes down, oh, quite frequently. But, of course, she has a husband so she's not as free to come and go. They're both retired. And the ladies in this building are very good. If Anne is away, they'll stop in, see that I'm okay.

I did know people in days gone by in nursing homes. My sister-in-law was in one up at Arbutus Street. She was there quite a long time, maybe two years. Her daughter was in Winnipeg in those days and had taken her mother down there to the home after my brother-in-law died. That's where they ended up. She thought maybe she'd like an apartment here. But I think she only stayed about three weeks; she didn't like it. So my sister-in-law came back here, and then took sick. She went blind and it was really hard for her. A housekeeper didn't work out. So then she went in the nursing home. Anne used to visit every day. I would go maybe once or twice a week to visit. In those days you couldn't get on the bus any time you felt like it. You had to count your pennies. It's not an ideal place.

I'm ready now, anytime, to pass along. I don't look forward to too much. Oh, I still have a game of bridge. My niece has a friend, and we usually have them over for dinner and a game, Anne and I. Sometimes we go to their place. Up until a few years ago I used to play at the community center, too. But I can't do that anymore, can't go there the same way I used to.

I'm ready. When you're not feeling okay, well, I'd be glad to just "go to sleep," just bow out. When you're not able to do things, life doesn't mean too much anymore. I can't go to church. I can't go to the Eastern Star meetings [a fraternal organization]. I'm a life member there but I can't go anymore. I can't sit there. Same for church. Last two times I went I passed out and they had to get the ambulance and take me to the hospital. Nothing much the matter with me except that I just couldn't take it. So I decided to stay home. It's just the last couple of years. I did really well up until then.

POSTSCRIPT

We all map our histories, orienting ourselves by the coordinates of "this place" at "that time." I've met few people of any age, however, who interpret their lives so assiduously in terms of place and time. But lodging and rooming houses, hotels and apartments, were not merely residences for the Grissoms. They were also a profession, a livelihood. The house on McDonald, the resort at Saskatchewan Beach, the litany of homes and apartments were the family's financial resource as well as its place of habitation.

Within this geography, the long social history of Heather Grissom's life shines through. Her early and short-lived independence in Edinburgh, cut short by her mother's need, is followed by the trip to Canada during World War I. There are the "dirty thirties," when even small, local stores failed because nobody had money to buy a plate and few people could afford a vacation.

Today the family home is an accepted ideal, almost a right. In Heather Grissom's day, however, it was a luxury. Many people rented across their lives or, if they had a home, it was a cottage industry with rooms to let to borders who needed a place to live, to get by. Similarly, although we assume work must be fulfilling, resenting jobs that don't offer gender equity and professional advancement, in Heather Grissom's world, work was first and foremost a way to pay the bills. Waiting on tables, caring for children, cleaning apartments, or renting rooms: for men and for women, work's purpose was more economic than social.

Feminists might read this story as an indictment of the rules that defined a woman's place across much of this century. I read it as the subtext of their assumptions. Yes, she cared for other people's children. She was a domestic who later owned the rooming house whose rooms she cleaned. But that did not make her less independent, less a partner in the life she and her husband constructed. For me, Heather Grissom's odyssey is a tale of strength and equality that is all the more modern for having begun in the early days of this century's first World War.

Of all the narrators in this collection, Heather Grissom was the only person I did not know before the interview began. Even though I first met Tim Harding on the day of our interview, we had talked several times by telephone. As importantly, my relationship with his wife, whom I had earlier interviewed and with whom I chatted at least twice a week, was an added introduction. This is, in short, a "true" interview, one in which there was no real personal referent except Dr. McArthur's suggestion to the Grissoms that they speak with me.

Indeed, it was largely at Bill McArthur's urging that Heather Grissom agreed to speak to me. Unlike Holly Treeson, she was not greatly interested in a new acquaintance, or in reviewing the episodes of her life with a stranger. She was, however, well aware of how unusual it is to find a physician willing to visit a fragile patient at home, to extend medical care from the office to the patient's own environment.[1] Our interview was thus as much her way of thanking him as it was of educating me.

In comparing this with other narratives—and especially that of Mrs. Bee, a lifelong family friend—I'm aware of the difference in quality and tone. Heather Grissom speaks to me less personally, more factually. The narrative does not include her private hopes and fears. Instead, there is the external range of her life, a story without emotional subtext. That says more, I believe, about the interview context than it does about her or her life. And by extension, I think, it speaks to the limits of the traditional academic or journalistic interview, the mining of strangers for their views. These works may be professional in style, but too often lack the intimacy that prior association might bring to a life history. This in no way diminishes my interest in Heather Grissom's narrative. It is simply to emphasize the degree to which the interpersonal context defines the type of data that is returned in an interview. And where the relations between subject and recorder are minimal, emotional revelations of necessity will be limited as a result.

NOTE

1. See, for example, William J. McArthur, Geriatric House Calls—Relic of the Past or Challenge of the Future? *Canadian Family Physician* (July 1991).

9

There Was a Crooked Man . . .

I balanced all, brought all to mind,
The years to come seemed waste of breath,
A waste of breath the years behind,
In balance with this life, this death.
William Butler Yeats, "An Irish Airman Foresees His Death"

Randolph and Jennifer Lamm moved to an apartment complex for seniors in Durham, North Carolina, when tensions became intolerable in the house they shared in Buffalo, New York, with their second oldest son, Walter, and his family. They now live perhaps two miles from their oldest son David's family, with whom relations are polite but distant. Known as a writer and photographer in his earlier years, Mr. Lamm later ran a well-known and well-regarded advertising company for many years.

In his maturity he was a fast and fluent talker, a direct and confident man in gait, speech, and perhaps action as well. Now he has mild but chronic emphysema that causes him to tire easily, "a touch of arthritis," and only partial recovery from a stroke. His right side remains weakened, affecting both his gait and the use of that hand. Further, he must sometimes pause and search for the phrasing of an idea that once would have been reflexive. "He searches for words, forgets names, forgets things," his son David said, adding dismissively and incorrectly, "but then, he always did that."

Like many seniors with a small financial reserve that, when interest rates were high, paid good dividends in the 1980s, the Lamms' disposable income has been eroded in the 1990s by declining interest rates. Yet, if he is to be believed, this is of no real importance to Randolph Lamm. Neither impoverished nor well-to-do, he is content to live the rest of his years in splendid silence.

The golden years? They're not golden, they're just years. I don't work, but my time is fully occupied doing nothing, very enjoyably. My health is still good. The only thing that's a problem is the right side, which is arthritis. The stroke doesn't really involve itself. It's just this one side, and the arthritis makes me walk kind of bad. But I'm still doing the same things I always did. See, I've gone through periods of great talk. And now I can go through a period of great silence. Because I don't talk. The only talking I do is saying, "I'll take this meat," or "I'll take this so and so." About the only contact I have with the outside world is doing that. And Jenny is hard of hearing, so we don't talk much. But I'm perfectly happy.

I have one strong belief, and it's that you should be able to do what you want to do. At any time, at any age, anywhere. Every person from the very bottom to the very top. When you go to the hospital, you see all these people there, these men sitting and thinking and worrying. Their wives are worrying, talking with their mothers or something. It's awful. But then you look at anything and it's mostly filled with people doing awful things. Killing each other. Not thinking. Being afraid. Making somebody afraid. I mean, look at all the people getting married today. People get married, they get divorced. They get married, they get divorced. And they can keep it up ten, twelve, fifteen times. Something is wrong somewhere.

Some people have never figured out what life is. Or nobody ever said anything to them at the right time. When I was a boy, we used to go visit these cousins in the country outside Charlotte, North Carolina. I was staying at their house one time and working in the fields. A little way up from their house was a log cabin. And the man who lived in that cabin was a Negro. One day I said something to him about, "Well, here we are alone, nigger." And he said, "Mr. Lamm, don't you know you don't say things like that to people?" And I said, "You don't?" And he said, "No, you don't." And I never did after that. But you wonder about it, because he wouldn't have said that to a lot of people. He'd just have accepted it. So I don't know what my lucky star has been or how it turned out this way. Maybe it was that I looked at my mother and my father and saw two separate beings. They were just people living together. I think so. They've both told me that it wasn't satisfying, that they had problems with other men and women. They weren't a functioning "thing," none of the people I knew were. So I kind of lived my own life by myself, and met the life that I wanted. Was my life different? I think so.

I never look forward. I never look backward. I don't read about any places that sound interesting to go to or that I can afford to go to. If I can't afford to go, I don't think of doing it. You see, I can't do too many things because I have very limited money. I have Social Security and, let's see, what income do I have? It's been reduced so much lately by falling interest rates. It used to be that I was getting $565 in interest per year, and then I had over $600. But now that's been cut in half. Plus a little over $12,000 a year from Social Security. I'm a little like those people you read about in the paper who are practically homeless. [*Laughs.*] I don't make enough money. Do I ever think about going back to work? Oh, no. My life has always been enjoyable, except having to get on that bus every day in the morning and go to work. I didn't like having to get on the bus every day, so I always went a half hour late.

My history? I was born in North Carolina in 1921. We moved to Durham when I was one. We lived in Durham until I was six. I lived right around the corner from where my son David lives now. In fact, he has the house around the corner from our old house. Then we moved to Connecticut, where I went to kindergarten, first, second—I skipped third grade—fourth, fifth, and half of sixth grade. Then we moved to Charlotte. We lived with my aunt for a couple of weeks, and then we moved into town. I finished junior high school there. We went up to Boston for the summer to settle my great-aunt's estate, and then we went to Buffalo. I finished high school. Then I had to take the last year over again, because of a girl. We had broken up and it was, ah, a bit of a mess. They didn't want me back in the same school, so I tried a school down in the city, and I didn't like it. Then I came back south to Concord, North Carolina, and finished the year.

Well, it was late that winter that I got pleurisy. Although you usually went to the hospital for it, I had a wonderful doctor and told him we could manage at home. So I stayed home, where he drained me twice[1]: once with a fine needle and once with a thick needle. I graduated from high school there. In fact, I got out of bed for the graduation. Then my family came down and took me home to Buffalo, where I was in bed all summer. Then it was time for college. I decided to go to Buffalo State College and take special courses. I had a nice interview with a woman there, and I took senior and junior courses. I was co-editor of a magazine they published. Wrote a full-length play they produced. That was what I was interested in—drama and English. I started going with another girl that winter and, ah, she was going to the same college, but she left the college and started working at the hospital. So I switched to the University of Buffalo for the second year, to be near her.

It was pretty awful. Except a course on "writing the novel." We kind of invented the course, the teacher and I. I was the only student in the course, and we just sort of consulted once every few weeks. I left college after that year and did nothing that summer—it was the middle of the Depression—and finally got a job with a company. I worked there about three months. Got another job with another company down in the city. I was a "stock record clerk." Then I left to go to a company next door called Thompson Products, where I wrote manuals explaining how to install various parts in machines that were for the army. Today you would call it technical writing. I worked there about a year, if you call it work. They'd have you work overtime some nights—everyone in the plant—for no reason. So everybody would stay down at the plant that night. During the day, I'd just wander off into the plant, and sometimes wander off and go downtown to a movie. [*Laughs.*]

I was making $50 a week, but I quit that job for a $35–a-week job at the newspaper, where I'd walk around town—you'd have a long list of products of newspaper advertisers—and check in the stores to see if they had those products. I'd go to different parts of the city and check the stores on this street and check that street for advertisers' products. And then after about three days of interviewing, I'd write a report. I did all types of interviews. Well, I kept that job for about a year. And I met Jenny during this time at her gallery. She and her sister had a gallery. Well, a salesman I'd seen who did some news advertising for them stopped by. It was Christmas time, and he got their ad. He was kind of a good friend of mine. He told me about them one day at lunch, so I stopped by the gallery. I fell in love with her when I saw her. I recognized that she was the girl in the painting that had won first prize out at the Annual Allentown Art show. Her father painted it. He was a good painter, and this girl in the painting just looked beautiful, this girl wearing a hat slanted down. The hat had some red in it. And then I walk into this gallery and see the girl! Did she immediately fall in love with me? No, of course not. That took about twenty years.

We'd gone down to New York that summer; she was on work for the gallery and things. Then I left the job at the newspaper after about a year and a half to go to South Bend, Indiana, where I stayed about three months. With Jenny. We weren't married or anything. Jenny and I told everybody we were married, that we had gotten married on the trip to New York that summer. Then, back in Buffalo, I went to a very interesting job at a company called Housier and Company, where I was advertising manager. And I got an apartment to live in. And I kept that job until they decided they wanted me to become a salesman, that they were doing away with their advertising department. They'd gotten an agency, et cetera. And, ah, then I went to work for Bethlehem Steel as editor of their magazine. And I got fired from that. The advertising manager called me about five o'clock one day. He wanted me to stop by and see him. I said, "I'll see you tomorrow. Why should I come out there? I'm not through here yet." I said, "Is there anything you have to tell me?" He said, "Yes." I said, "Well, what is it?" And he said, "You're fired." And I said, "Well, why didn't you tell me that before?" So he fired me, and I never went back. I had lots of jobs.

David was already born at that time, and Jenny was pregnant again. We spent most of the summer going around visiting people in North Carolina. I started to write a book. Then we flew down to Mexico, went to Mexico to live.[2] We went down on a Pullman. First we went to Mexico City and then took the plane to Acapulco. From there we were to fly into this little town. We were going to stay in a little town down on the coast. Well, we couldn't get a plane for a week, so we stayed in Acapulco until we could. Finally we got there. We walked through the town and it was so beautiful. I still remember a church and a lot of fleecy clouds in layers up above it. We had a big warehouse of a room with nothing in it, except two camp cots for three people: me, Jennifer, and David. Well, Jenny was crying and didn't like it. So I went down and found the place where you bought tickets and was able to get tickets back to Mexico City for the next day. The next morning we went back to the airfield, waited until a plane came, and flew out, flew to Mexico City.

Looked up a friend there whom we'd met on the train coming down, the head of Reuters News Agency. Somebody at his place knew of a place in Cuernavaca. Somebody had a house there, so we went down to see it. Rented it. And we stayed there until Christmas. Jenny was going to have this baby and we wondered if we should stay down beyond this time or if we should go back right after Christmas. Well, we went back right after Christmas. She flew home and I rode home on the bus and finished the novel. It was horrible. David made a copy of it for me this year. It was buried in some old file.

Then I went through a number of jobs. Jenny had Walter, but we couldn't find a place to live. So Jenny lived at her family's place and I lived at mine. I'd go out and see them on weekends. We finally got a place way out in the country, a one-room house. Horrible place. We stayed there for a few weeks and finally found a place in town and moved to that.

I was losing jobs and getting jobs and what not. Never a huge salary, except when I was ad manager at Housier. That was the best salary, when it looked like I was going to be a brilliant young man making over $350 a month. Anyway, the company I was working for fired me because the president's son, who had been working downstairs kind of running the office, wanted something better. And the only space in the building was in my office, so I got fired. But I kept writing a magazine for them, a weekly magazine, and I did this on contract for over a year, a year and a half. Well, that's what we lived on.

After that there were several jobs with typesetters and what not. You know, I never seemed to do the job, because the job didn't take any work. Like, at one company I was supposed to be a type salesman. I didn't know how you got type customers. There were only two typesetters in town and they were both always working. So I serviced the accounts, delivered the jobs, brought them back, and what not. It was fine. I had that one for quite a while.

This house that we had lived in, well, the second year there we found that the people were charging us too much, so we got a lower rent for another year, negotiated about half off from the previous year. Anyhow, then we left that place and went to the housing projects. We got in because Jenny's family had a friend who was in charge of that and a million other things. We lived in the projects for a number of years. It was wonderful. It had a nice yard out front and we'd go out and bat the baseball and there were big bridges nearby where the youngest, Allan, my youngest, would climb underneath the bridge, then up and over to the other side. He wouldn't have gotten up on the thing to begin with if I'd been watching! You never do things like that when the adults watch.

There in the projects I started the Film Society. We showed three series of films the first year—one in the fall, one in the winter, and one in the spring. We'd gotten a projector. The fellow who lived next door to us—Nick Zabatisi—and I, we stopped smoking and saved the money for a couple of months to buy it. I think the projector cost us $255 or something like that. It was a real early sound projector, and another friend—Harry Schultz—he was going to get films for us from Eastman House. Well, that didn't work out well, so I started renting films from different places. And we had this small apartment in the projects, but it was packed with people sitting around the living room as we projected onto a six-foot screen. Then we decided to show films in an outside place for the public. We moved them to the Masonic Hall.

So I was busy. I had a job and the Film Society to run, program notes to write. A family. Friends. So it was quite full. And I was taking photographs. All this time, from the time we went to Mexico, I was taking photographs. You can't find any of my photographs now because I always sent the original negatives off—and they never sent them back from the editors. So the pictures just vanished. But I won first prize when the American Photographer had a competition. I bought a good camera with the winnings from that, bought a Contax. I won first prize, along with three or four other photographers, but I won all the way down the line. I won lots of prizes. I mean, my pictures were very heavy in the show. And that was really the only competitive photographic competition that's been held in this country—nationally—that anybody could enter. Some of the other winners are big photographers today.

Anyway, the first year of running the Film Society, the program was good. The second was good. But by the third we weren't making enough money to keep paying the Masonic Hall for space. So we had to move. We moved to a place across the street for the last series. Then I started showing the films at home again. I showed films more or less once a week for twenty years. It was a good film society, and the first of its kind. When it started it was the only thing of its kind anywhere in the country. And it kept going and going and going until, many years later, when the kids were grown and married, I quit my job and went to Mexico again. But that was later.

We stayed there in the projects for many years. I was a successful advertising man when we left. I'd finally gotten a job with an art studio, selling type. I was making a good living. In fact, in one summer month I made $450. We went out to the beach for summer vacations. I got horribly sunburned on one of them. After I had my own advertising studio, we moved to the suburb of Amherst.

We took the kids to Mexico one summer on a trip. It was a wonderful trip. We went to Merida. Then we took the bus to Villahermosa. We walked into the hotel and they said, "Did you see the sign outside?" And I said, "No, we didn't see any sign outside. What do you mean?" And we went out and there was a big sign, "Welcome Jennifer and Randolph Lamm." This was the first year they had opened the road to Villahermosa and down through that area. It was kind of virgin territory for people. From there, we took a plane and flew up to San Cristobal las Casas [*in the southern province of Chiapas*]. Couldn't land in San Cristobal because it was overcast, and so we had to fly down the mountain. Then we took a car up. It was a brand new road. It had just been finished from Oaxaca down to the border, and from the bottom road up to this mountain. I was scared to death! In fact, I never wanted to go back down.

But we traveled and took jeeps to all the local festivals in the area. It was a wonderful trip. When we got to San Cristobal it was completely different than it had been down on the coast. In Merida, the kids said, "If it's all like this, we want to go home." But they loved San Cristobal. Then we took a bus to Oaxaca. And we loved Oaxaca! That's when we started collecting Mexican folk art. We took a bus to Mexico City and a first-class Mexican plane to the United States, and then flew to Buffalo. The kids were teenagers, so that's about thirty-five years ago, around 1960.

We went down to Mexico several times after that with the kids, and we ran the studio in Buffalo until the kids got out of college. David had gone east to school but came home with his new wife, Christine, to be with us that summer. Walter had gotten his librarian's degree and was going to work in the fall. Allan was married and living a few blocks away. And it happened one day that we bought a car to drive down to Mexico. I'd given a year's notice at my studio, and we set things up so the other partners in the business could take over. Then the day came, the kids packed my car, and they packed their trucks with their things, and the next morning everybody—shoosh!—in all directions. This was retirement. That was in 1970.

After two years, I saw that we wouldn't be able to make things work in Mexico because we'd spent a lot of money on the house there and prices were zooming up. So we decided to come home. Walter was going to move back to Buffalo and get a job there. So come home we did, and got back Christmas Eve. Walter had a small apartment, and we stayed with them—Walter and his wife, Susan—until we could go the next day to see a house that I'd had them buy for me. I'd never seen it before that. I went and saw the house. It was a fine house, needed a lot of work. It wasn't difficult at all. It was fun. We moved in. Walter and Susan moved in. We'd lived with Walter and Susan all through their college years. Then Allan moved back in. And so we were all in the house: Allan and his wife, Jill, Walter and Susan and their daughter, Martha, and me. And Jennifer.

I looked for a job on and off for a year. When I first got to Buffalo, I went to Katrell Studios and asked for a job. We'd known each other for some years. I mean, we'd been competing for the same work when I had my own studio. But by this time my customers and his customers had mixed in such a way that it wasn't of any value to him to hire me. Then, a year later, he ran an ad in the paper: "Young apprentice salesman. $10,000." I called him and said, "Pay me $12,000, and I'll come take your job." And that was the job I had for the years I remained in business. Toward the end, our company had tough times. The clients had started doing their advertising in-house, so we didn't get much business. I was the only one making any money for them at the end. The company closed. Then I retired and we came down here.

There were difficulties that had been growing at the house. Walter's wife, Susan, didn't like my smoking—although Walter used to smoke all the time. But he'd kind of quit, except for occasional cigars. She'd take her family into the living room after dinner, away from my smoking. And we just kind of grew apart. We also wanted to get out of the snow and the ice, so one day we just happened to come down here. We came down and looked. We found an apartment, a place to live that looked very nice. And we had just enough furniture for it, so we had it shipped down. Stayed there until we moved to this apartment. We didn't move here because David's here. But we wouldn't have moved here otherwise.

POSTSCRIPT

Increasingly blind, plagued by the effect of several strokes complicated by his diabetes, an elderly and failing Jean Paul Sartre was asked how he felt about his condition.[3] "I'm not stupid," he told his questioner and companion, Simone de Beauvoir. "But I'm empty." His writing was done, his arguments complete. He was, as Mr. Lamm says he is, in a floating period of present silence, of existence without future direction. In commenting on Sartre at this point in his life, Kathleen Woodward wrote, in *Aging and Its Discontents*, that "He cannot locate himself in the social world. He has no place . . . his body does not serve him as a refuge or a shelter."[4]

The same might be said, today, of Mr. Lamm. Sartre told Simone de Beauvoir he liked to sit "doing nothing," enjoyed time spent not in anxiety or inactivity but with contentment and at rest. It is, perhaps, what Randolph Lamm calls his "period of great silence." Whether more attention from family or friends, more social support, would animate him today is an open question. The support is not there, however, except from his wife. With her he shares both mundane daily conversation and a palpable, joint history that now spans more than fifty years.

What is remarkable is not Randolph Lamm's bald statement of disengagement, of a present divorced from past work or future expectation, but its uniqueness in this and other volumes about the lives of the elderly. But then, he is in any age an unusual person. Mr. Lamm seems to be a man for whom distance—from others and from normal contexts—has been a mode of being. Work was irrelevant, he says, except as a means of earning the money he needed to live. He took little pleasure from it and developed few strong personal ties from the people he met in his mundane working life. His passions were photography, writing, and film. Today, however, he belongs to neither photographic clubs nor film societies. It is as if the silence he describes is a minimalist canvas he consciously created, one in which the foreground is obscured and the background muted. Perhaps it is a palimpsest whose surface image is painted on and thus obscures older, historical images.

Throughout this narrative Randolph Lamm uses the first person singular rather than the first person plural—"I" instead of a "we"—which would include his wife, children, and coworkers. "I had to go to South Bend, Indiana, where I stayed about three months," he says of a trip with his wife to avoid the ignominy of their first child being born out of wedlock. "I got an apartment to live in," he says about their return to Buffalo. But the new apartment was for his family as well. The births of their sons David and Walter are almost ignored in a narrative subsumed in the history of work and travel. The intergenerational problems, which resulted in the departure of the Lamms from their home in Buffalo, problems that Jennifer Lamm describes with sadness, are dismissed here as simply "growing apart" and a disagreement over Mr. Lamm's tobacco habit.

Jennifer Lamm remembers her children packing their things, the dispersal of the goods—and the people—who had filled her house and homes for twenty years. Mr. Lamm, on the other hand, remembers that "the kids [not "our kids" or "my kids"] packed my [not "our"] car" for the trip to Mexico. In today's climate, none of this makes him a sympathetic character. And yet, to see his strengths, one must see Randolph Lamm in perspective. His tale does not do him justice. To complete this story it is necessary to listen to his wife's narrative of these years and this relationship.

NOTES

1. That is, draining his lungs was done at the Lamm household rather than in the hospital, where this procedure is more typically carried out.

2. At this time Mexico was what Paris had been in the early 1930s, an inexpensive and amenable location for relatively impecunious artists seeking time and freedom to paint or write.

3. Simone de Beauvoir, *Adieux: A Farewell to Sartre*, Trans. Patrick O'Brian (New York: Penguin, 1984).

4. Kathleen Woodward, *Aging and Its Discontents: Freud and Other Fictions* (Bloomington: Indiana University Press, 1991), 177–179.

10

. . . Who Walked a Crooked Mile

No marble, no conventional phrase;
By his command these words are cut:
Cast a cold eye
On life, on death,
Horseman, pass by!
                    William Butler Yeats, "Under Ben Bulben"

Unlike the Hardings, whose perception of their shared years was complimentary, the Lamms present radically different interpretations of their life together. Not surprisingly, for two whose historical perspectives differ, their present evaluations are similarly distinct. Jennifer Lamm does not appreciate either the isolation of their current life or the prospect of a future based on a continuing if unchanging present.

But as a person who has battled partial deafness for decades, the "great silence" her husband enjoys is, for her, the continuation of a physical silence she knows too well. And while her vision is fine, a family history of retinal detachments has given her a fear of sight impairments, of the potential for another physical disability that would further limit her world.

This may explain, in part, her enthusiasm for euthanasia. "The man in Michigan" to whom she refers is Jack Kevorkian. At the time of this interview he was beginning to gain his present notoriety. The mechanics of suicide that she discusses—the efficacy of various pills and dosages, the use of an asphyxiating plastic bag—are gleaned from the literature of the Hemlock Society, which advocates the legalization of assisted suicide.

Whorem I was middle-aged I still felt young, you know? I mean, I knew consciously what middle age was. Thirty-five is middle age, thirty-five to fifty-five years. But thirty-five is still *young.* Old age is completely different. Actually, there are a lot of things I like about it. In many respects it's a big liberation for me from a lot of things. I no longer feel bad that I'm not gorgeous and beautiful, like I always wished that I was. I never thought I looked like what I saw in the mirror. I always thought I really was much more sophisticated, much more beautiful than that. Now, I'm not trying to impress anybody with either my wit or my looks, or anything. Personal vanity is gone, pretty much. Well, I don't want to look sloppy or slovenly. But that personal vanity part, it's a good thing to be rid of. It's too bad it happened so late in my life.

I guess I've become liberated in my old age. I've certainly become much more aware of women's liberation and so forth and so on. I'm amazed it took me so long to get over the idea that a woman was somehow less than a man, to realize that these people are right. That's liberating. I don't know whether Randolph has mellowed or if he's just gotten used to my liberation. But I don't just accept things he says anymore—and of course he doesn't say as much as he used to. Every once in a while he'll come up with one of his old "Randolph-isms," as we call them, and I'll just laugh. You know, something like I'm a D. H. Lawrence woman who's up to her neck in the pit and the Angel Gabriel comes along and . . . all that kind of crap. Now I just laugh at him.

There's the huge responsibility that you have when the children are growing up, but that's over now. I don't worry about them anymore. Well, I still worry! I mean, when my daughter-in-law Christine didn't come this morning to the YMCA swimming class, I thought, "Oh my! What happened? Did something happen?" But I'm pretty confident, and that's a relief. At the same time, it's kind of sad. You don't have all those close connections. They don't rely on you so much. So it's a big difference.

And physically, I *feel* different. I'm no longer as agile. I don't have the energy I used to have. I'm perfectly willing to take it easy and not feel guilty. There's much less guilt. In fact, to heck with it. I used to tell my son David that he could put "mea culpa" on my gravestone because I felt that everything that was wrong was my fault. I don't feel that way anymore. Now they can put: "Horseman, pass by!" I've taken to Yeats. [*Laughs.*][1]

When I start to think about it, I think there are so many things that are sad. You don't have the kids around, you don't have all these connections, and so on. I miss my family in Buffalo, where Randolph and I met and married and lived for years. We left thinking that the kids there, Walter and Susan, didn't like having us around anymore, but now we know in retrospect that the problems between us were really a matter of their kids growing up. I wouldn't mind living with Walt and Susan again once their kids are grown. That is, if I were still in good health, and once they have their little farm. They are looking forward to a farm, and Walter can retire in just a few years. But I'd hate to live with them if they had to take care of me.

Burden is a word I hate, and it *is* a burden if you have to take care of somebody all the time. Burden and dependence and pain. Oh, yeah. If I started having a big problem that involved chronic pain, I would opt out if I could. It would have been hard to take care of my father after I retired. I don't see how I could have taken care of a parent and been married, too. That would have been a terrible burden. You're not free. I think the issue is dependence versus independence. I lived with Walt and Susan for fifteen years. I don't mind being dependent in terms of having a place to live. But then to be dependent on them in terms of them having to take care of me? Put diapers on me and change me, things like that? I think I'd rather use the pills and kill myself.

Just growing older irritates me, even though I think I'm as well off as I could possibly be. What would I change? I might change where I live because being in North Carolina in the middle of summer, it's so hard to go out. Because it's hot and muggy, going out is miserable. I don't know where, though, would be a better place to live. Because we don't drive, we need the closeness of stores and things. We go to movies that are within walking distance. Film has been important to us. So we walk up to the Rialto [a local, old-style movie house]. It's a good little walk. Or we walk over to the Mystic Valley cinemas [in a mall], which is another good walk. When we first came down here, it was a lot easier than it is now—the walks. And that was just five years ago. The movies that I *must* see become less imperative than they used to be, because of the walk. It seems like the theaters are further, although of course that isn't it. I realize that.

We used to belong to a music society over in the university district, another good little walk, but I no longer feel like it is an automatic thing that I buy the tickets, that we *have* to go. They used to get the Juilliard String Quartet and people like that, but they don't have the money anymore or the groups have become more expensive. So the concert series has become more interesting to some people, in some respects, because of the younger groups coming in to play, but it's nothing I feel compelled to attend. The walk is what bothers me. Of course we could take a cab, but I'm married to the tightest man on the face of the earth, a man who doesn't believe in cabs! I guess the new liberation doesn't extend to things like that.

I never thought I'd get to be this age. Never. When I was young I thought, "Well, if I reach forty." Forty years was far off. Then it was, well, fifty years. But finally you stop thinking about it. You just naturally grow older. My father was in his nineties and Randolph's grandfather was in his nineties when they died. So there are a lot of people in our families who have lived long lives. On my mother's side, everybody died young. They were all fifty, fifty-five years. I used to have a lot of old aunts who I didn't like very much. I didn't have any respect or disrespect for them *because* of age. I just didn't much like them.

Now it's amazing to me to think how young some of the people were that I thought of as so much older. They must have been in their thirties and forties when I was little. It's hard for me to even think that I thought in those terms. My grandkids don't have any respect for us because of age. What feelings they have come from liking us, I think, or disliking us. But I don't think the age thing has had anything to do with it.

There's another big difference when you're old—you're closer to *ceasing.* And all those things you think of in the abstract when you're younger become very pertinent. I mean, consciousness is everything, as far as I'm concerned. And once consciousness is gone, that's it. You're very close to that understanding as you get older. If nobody else died and I had to think of cessation, I would be very upset. But it happens to everybody. So you have to appreciate everything said over the hundreds and thousands of years about cessation. I think it's age, how old you are, how you *feel.* It's reading about it, too. The constant worry about Alzheimer's—which is my principal worry—or losing complete control of your being. After a certain age, after sixty-five, you pass the cutoff. We've always been aware there was a cutoff there because that's when you start receiving Social Security. There's a lot of discussion now about older people, too. They're making big stories about it, about aging.

Control is what it's all about. The children can try to get even for all the things you did to them when they were little. They have you in their power now. [*Laughs.*] Like, David used to make me walk so fast when he was grown up. And he used to say when we walked together, "Well, you used to make *me* walk too fast when I was little." I'm not sure I want to be in my kids' hands when I'm old! It's primarily because of my mother, I think. They didn't call it Alzheimer's then, but she became . . . nothing. She couldn't eat. She wasn't even like an animal because even a dog knows how to eat and so forth. That really has upset me tremendously. And then you read that it's a hereditary disease.

They had retired to Florida and she was kind of strange before they went, like she would tell you stories over and over. They retired to Sarasota and bought a little house. They sold their old house for some low sum of money—$35,000 or something. And there were acres of land! And then they allowed the people to whom they sold the house to send them so much money a month, so they wouldn't have to go through a bank and pay interest.

At any rate, Mother's own husband, my father, had her put into a nursing home. This was in Florida. He didn't think he could afford anything else, so he put her into a state hospital, which I found devastating. But I didn't do anything about it. I went down once to see how they were and it was pretty sad. She was still able to talk some of the time, converse some. And after that she just became . . . nothing. But she knew she was in hospital. My other sisters went more than I did. I had a horror of things like that. So that's why it worries me, but it doesn't worry me constantly.

Years and years ago I was hired to take care of an old woman who was over ninety. She was almost blind and had a hearing aid, but she was a marvelous lady. Her daughter worked at the university in Buffalo and couldn't come home to make lunch and so forth and so on. So I did that. I went up there from about ten o'clock until two o'clock every day. And they paid me. I probably wouldn't have done this if I hadn't gotten paid. The old lady finally had a stroke and she was taken to the hospital. I went to visit her. They had put all these things [electrodes] on her head—a ninety-three-year-old woman—and she couldn't understand them, what they were saying to her. She couldn't *hear* them. She couldn't see. And the doctor said, "We have to find out if she's had a stroke." But why? *Why* did they have to know? I mean, she was ninety-three years old, or something like that.

She was speaking German. She could speak English, but German was what she was speaking. The black help at the hospital were all calling her by her first name, and she couldn't understand them, what they were saying to her. I was just appalled by the whole thing. In the first place, the doctor should never have allowed this to happen. All these tests, these electrodes attached to her head, without her understanding what was going on! And then to call this dignified old lady, this very elegant old lady, by her first name. Me? I just held her hand. And she clutched *my* hand.

I called her daughter and said, "This is just the most appalling thing." Of course she didn't like me for saying this. She didn't like to be told that they weren't treating her mother well. After all, it wasn't my business or anything. But it was just awful. They were treating her like a thing! Then they put her in a fancy nursing home where the help was still like that—familiar.

No matter how much you pay in places like that, they don't have elegant nurses.

Randolph would say it isn't important. If he were in bad shape and they started calling him "Randolph," I don't think he would care. But I would.

So I think euthanasia should be much simpler. I think we should be able to talk to a doctor—to somebody—and say "when." After all, *everybody* dies. It's just absurd to have a whole industry around nursing homes and people being kept alive in horrible conditions *just because they're alive.* There has to be some cutoff of consciousness that marks an end to life. I should be able to say when, but now I have to stick my head in the oven or something.

I much prefer the man in Michigan [*Jack Kevorkian*] who does something about it, the one with the suicide machine. I've copied down a little list of how much you need of various drugs to kill yourself. I don't like the thought of having to use the plastic bag at the same time. Just to make sure, you're supposed to put your head in a plastic bag to cut the oxygen. And also, I worry that swallowing all this stuff you might just vomit it up. But I'm still in favor of it, euthanasia.

I thought Allan would be the easiest to ask for help, to get the materials because he goes to Mexico so often and these drugs are quite available in Mexico. In fact, Allan could get almost anything. He has enough friends in various spots. I've asked him, but he's said no. "You mean you'd take them yourself and leave me with Randolph?" he asked. "Or give them to Randolph when you're tired of him?" Now, he's sort of joking, but not altogether. Also, he's not that convinced that death is the end. He likes to think that the spirit remains. Now my son Walter, in Buffalo, he has a lot of good friends who are doctors, and he said, "I can get you the pills anytime you want them." But he hasn't done it.

I've talked this over with Randolph, who doesn't seem to be the least bit interested in a suicide pact. What I said to Randolph was, "Eighty-five, let's make eighty-five years our cutoff date." But he just laughs. He's not even seventy-five, and he's not in great health. I would be perfectly willing. There was an article about a couple that just decided at a certain time to kill themselves—and did. With no fuss. And their families were supportive and so forth and so on. That's what I think would be ideal. Well, what's ideal is dying in your sleep with no pain and no problems. But the big question is *when* is the right time for it? You like to think that if all goes well, you might as well stay alive a little longer. So you don't want to have a cutoff date that is too soon. But what's the right time? I suppose it's when you're still in good spirits without any incipient misery. I don't want to make it too early. There are too many interesting things. It's like Stendhal, you know? He didn't want to die because he wanted to know what would happen, how things would turn out.

I see this primarily as an elderly concern. I never thought of it as anything else. Well, I *always* thought I could jump off a bridge. That's what I was going to do when I was pregnant the first time. I was going to go jump off the high-level bridge because, back then—in the 1940s—there was no legalized abortion and to say you were unmarried and pregnant was . . . in my family? No. So suicide seemed to be the only alternative. But I didn't jump off the bridge, obviously. I did go to Indiana.

I think suicide should be legitimate at any age. I think if people want to kill themselves bad enough, they do. But you hate to think of kids doing it because they haven't had the chance to think things through. My favorite granddaughter swallowed a bottle of aspirin, but then she went downstairs and told her parents. So then they rushed her to hospital, where they pumped out her stomach. I'm sure she's glad that nothing more serious happened because now she's fallen in love, and today life for her is wonderful and beautiful. So, as I said, she rushed down and told them, and I didn't jump off the bridge. But is life all that grand? Is it that we've had a moment of consciousness, what we call consciousness? Is it all that valuable? I don't know. But I didn't jump off the bridge and in retrospect, am I glad? Oh, yes!

We met, Randolph and I, when I was still twenty-two, the year I had David. The year I almost jumped off the bridge. We met in my gallery. My sister and I had an art gallery, and Randolph walked in one day. He was selling advertising space for the local newspaper. Randolph was a scream. I never thought I'd marry him in a million years. I mean, if I hadn't gotten pregnant, I wouldn't have. At least, that's what I say now, but who knows? He wore this big Borsolino hat. He was very skinny, skate narrow. And he talked like Hemingway, right out of Hemingway was the way he talked. I thought he was a scream. He became persistent. We were quite young. I certainly never projected this.

And I just gave up everything. I put myself in Randolph's hands, more or less. My sister and I still ran the gallery, and Randolph would get very upset with some of the things she did, even though my father was the one paying all the bills and so on. Randolph would order me around. So I quit. I stopped. It would have been hard for me to go to work in those days. I felt strongly I should be with the kids. It was a mess, one of those messes.

If I had had any sense, I would have stood up more for myself. But I just accepted him and his ideas. I mean, the fact that we didn't listen to modern jazz because *he* didn't like it. There were certain modern writers that he liked. One day he threw a copy of T. S. Eliot at my head! And I just accepted Randolph, which was absurd. But he was pretty remarkable in many respects. He brought life to the house. He brought books home. I was interested in folk music, and God! Every folk record that was ever made beginning with Burl Ives he'd bring home for me. Early on, because we didn't have the money for a sitter and I couldn't leave the kids, he'd go to a movie by himself. If he thought I'd like it, he'd insist that a friend come and take me to the theater while he stayed home with the kids. And he brought people to the house. In the early days, he brought people home who were interesting, and they'd become friends of the whole family.

It was self-imprisonment almost, if you want to call it that. You know, in many respects I did it to myself. Randolph strongly believed in women's rights in spite of all his D. H. Lawrence stuff. "Imprisoned" isn't the right word. I shouldn't have said it. In retrospect, I think I would have been a great English teacher, or student. I could have done anything I wanted. And Randolph used to try and get me to write. I did do book reviews for the newspapers. He wanted me to write stories and so on. So, in retrospect, I think I might have been a different kind of person. But who knows? It's impossible to say.

Later, I lived with Walt and Susan for fifteen years. Walter and Susan, Allan and his wife, and Randolph and I bought a house together in Buffalo. Then Allan and his wife were gone, almost from the very start. They left after the first year, divorced. We started out being completely interdependent, and then it got so that Susan cooked one night and I cooked the next night. We had certain specific rules that we followed. It was a very interesting business. If I were a writer, I'd write about it. Susan had been, you know, like a daughter. Walter was young and in high school when he first met Susan, and I was kind of her mentor. Ah, it was a wonderful relationship for me because I had no daughters and Susan was delightful.

We wrote back and forth when I went to Mexico, and I got wonderful letters from her. Randolph and I first retired, for a time, to Mexico. And she was my best friend for a long time after I got back from Mexico and we were in the house together again. We suffered through the business with Allan and Joyce, their divorce, but Susan was my friend. Then when her kids, especially her oldest daughter, began to grow up, the situation very subtly began to change. I don't know whether I got jealous of the relationship between them—Susan and her daughter—but I became like her *mother.* So there was a conflict that hadn't been there before. And what had been a lovely relationship developed a lot of prickles, bad feelings.

That situation kind of fell apart finally. And by then Randolph had turned sixty-five and he'd gotten fired from his last job. Well, the man he worked for went out of business. The thought of going out and trying to get work again at the age of sixty-five was more than Randolph was willing to do. And so it seemed like a good cutoff point. I think he probably would have continued to work if the company hadn't closed because he was interested in what he was doing and he had these young friends, young art directors. He never seemed to have much in common with the older ones. They seemed to have suffered him. But he really never liked to work. I mean, he retired the first time when he was fifty. If he could have done it, Randolph would never have gone to work at all.

That's when we moved here to Durham. When I look back, it was a bad time to move. I lost out on the kids growing up in Buffalo, the crucial period of their growing up. At the same time, it was that crucial period that really forced us to move. I thought one good thing about moving was that I'd get to know David and Christine's two kids. But I feel that—and this may be wrong—that they don't have much interest in us. I feel bad about it. I feel quite bad that I don't see them very often. Charlie, the youngest, I don't know at all. And I can't *hear* their oldest, Donald, because he sort of talks real soft and mumbles. I can't hear on one side, you know. I had it for years. When we first moved down here, I couldn't hear anything Donald said. But I didn't want to keep having to say, "I can't hear you." Kids at that age, they're not prone to listen, you know. It's a hard age.

Because we used to write back and forth, I was much closer to David when I was living in Buffalo, almost, than I am now that I'm down here in the same city. Now he seldom calls and comes to see us even less. I think partly it's that he's busy and partly it's, well, I don't know. We told him we wouldn't bug him when we came down here. I don't think Randolph feels it. He calls David when he has something to say. I think if we were hurt or sick, David would come. I think his wife, Christine, has to remind him to call the "old folks."

I know I'm old, but I don't think we're "old folks." And I resent certain things. I resent that I don't have the same relationship with my kids as I did before. It's a bad word, but I suppose "resent" is how you feel. You want them to accept you, but at the same time I've found myself getting angry because David's telephone will be off the hook when I telephone. He does that when he is working, takes the phone off the hook. And I'll say to myself, "Hey, you know, this is your mother calling!" Then I have to laugh because, good God! Why should I have more access to him than anyone else? And it gets me real mad that they—Susan and Walt—don't write from Buffalo.

I've told them, "I *need* the letters because, over the phone, I can't hear you." When I have a letter, I can read it over again, I can *see* it. But they're not writers. So I get kind of mad and say, "Well, *I'm* not going to call *them*."

Still, I feel very close to them. My middle granddaughter there, Donna, she wrote a lot this past winter when she was away at college. But now that she's gotten home to Buffalo and her love is there with her, well, she hasn't written much. And *that* makes me mad. Well, mad with a smile on my face. You don't give up that love. You never stop being a parent. I know Randolph's father, when he had a sixty-year-old daughter, he said he was still a parent and she was still a daughter. She called him "Daddy" and things like that. I don't think you ever stop.

There's a little bench down at the front of the apartment building. I was sitting there the other day when Randolph came walking up. He has this one hip that juts out since his stroke, and I thought, "There was a crooked man who walked a crooked mile." And I said to him, "We're just like the people in the nursery rhymes." He doesn't like it. He can't do things with his hand and it bothers him. But he seems to take it well. He doesn't bitch about it all the time. What can you do if you don't have some kind of humor about it all? This morning, he couldn't see the bottom of his foot! He has a wart, or whatever it's called, on the bottom of his foot, and I have to put this stuff on it that he got from the doctor. And I said to him, "Boy, I'd feel terrible if I couldn't see the bottom of my own foot!" Then I thought, well, maybe it's not all that easy. It bothers me to see him like this.

It's sad to lose your hearing. I go to this thing in the morning at the Y, swimming, and afterwards these women in the group are all talking and I can hear little bits and pieces, but that's all. I get this kind of sweet smile on my face. Folks are saying things, talking and laughing. And I'm not hearing it. So I'm not participating. A lot of it is stuff I'd just as leave not hear, of course . . . gossip.

But still, I'd rather lose my hearing than my sight. That's another thing that worries me, going blind, because then you can't be in control, you know? Things can happen to you that you can't control at all because you can't see. I have retinal problems. I've had laser surgery that's supposed to have corrected the problem, the doctor said. Glaucoma and things like that can come with age, too. Cataracts. Not being able to see would be pretty devastating. I can turn my hearing aid off and not worry about things. I hear well enough without it to not feel too isolated.

Now, we see no one. My social life is up there at the Y, three mornings a week, and there are neighbors I talk to. Randolph hardly talks to them at all. I think he's shy. He is. To most people he doesn't have anything to say, doesn't have small talk. But we see no one. We have no friends down here. And I don't feel it as a terrible lack. Thirty years ago we had friends. We've had friends all along, close friends, friends for dinners, and friends we could do things with, like trips to New York. He used to invite people home from work every now and then for dinner. But they were mostly work-related friends. And then there was the film society he started, people interested in film, and they became friends.

Still, we're very lucky. We have enough money. We sold the house in Buffalo to give us a little cushion, and Randolph had a little cushion from work. I used to think—when we first thought of retiring—I thought we could live on $250 a month, which is what I thought we'd get in Social Security. I counted on it. That's what I thought we'd live on. And you know, that's what we are living on, pretty much. We do have a little cushion in the bank besides, but I figured out that even here, in this apartment, we could live on what we get. We get $1,248 a month. Obviously, we're getting a bit more out of it than we might have put into it. I am. Certainly I am. I didn't work long enough. But Randolph did and, if Randolph died, I'd get his Social Security payments as well.

I went through the Depression, but I don't remember them talking about Social Security. Was it under Roosevelt? Yeah, but it was before I was working. I don't remember hearing any talk about it. No one in my family was a Democrat. They were strictly Republican. I do remember my father being very angry about the fact that he had to pay in even when he was the head of a business, that he was supposed to put so much money in. He didn't like that. But he changed a lot as he got older. My father was a staunch Christian Scientist who ended up not being a Christian Scientist at all. He ended up going to doctors and so forth and so on. He just kind of accepted it, I think. You get scared and worried, I think. Social Security, too. Now it's just accepted. He broke his hip a couple of times. All kinds of terrible things happened to him. And you come to accept medicine and anything that gives you some relief.

I think if Randolph weren't here I would travel more. All my brothers and sisters are alive. One sister's in Detroit. My sister Jill and her husband, Gary, are in Montreal and Amsterdam—they have apartments in both places—and my brother Robert is in Phoenix. I'd travel more to see them, and I think I'd spend chunks of time with them. Randolph doesn't want to travel. Jill and Gary invited us to use their apartment in Amsterdam, where they live part of the year, but Randolph wouldn't go. I didn't insist because I didn't really like Amsterdam when I visited it once for a week. But Randolph hasn't wanted to go to Montreal either. And they're very friendly people, although, I must say, they're hard to stay with for very long. I'm sure I'd visit my sister Marion with whom I had the gallery, but her husband and Randolph don't get along at all. This goes way, way back to when we all were in our twenties and Randolph, he resented so many things about my sister and the rest of my family from when we were young. It seems to me that he resented my interest in them, but I'm not sure. I could be wrong about that. This has been a big problem because my sister and I were very, very close. We haven't been that close for all these years, but I think we could be again.

Advice? Save your money so you can live well. I'd hate to be old and poor and really worried about money. So far we don't feel that way. We can travel a little bit, and we get what we want. We can rent movies, which we don't do as often as we should. If we want to buy a book or something, we do it. I would hate to be old and poor and dependent. That's what I would say: work for your independence. The woman at the library just retired. Yesterday was her last day of work. She's a clerk/librarian, I think. And I said, "This is going to be great!" And she said, "Well, I'm looking forward to it." And I said, "I've never read so much in my life as I have in these past few years. All I do is read." And she says, "I'm going to take some courses and I'm going to do this and that."

I've thought of that too, going over to the university and auditing some courses. But I can't hear well enough to take in a lecture. I *can* read the books. I'd rather read about these things anyway. I volunteered at the Arboretum and it was enjoyable, but it was too difficult for me to get there easily. It was kind of a mess. If there were a better public transit system, things would be easier. I might do more—volunteer at the museum, for example—but there's no way to get to that art museum easily. So that's that.

POSTSCRIPT

On a superficial level, the Lamms are an archetypal couple, conforming to stereotypes of male and female perceptual states. In *A Place of Her Own*, for example, Carol Gilligan argues that men and women have been so trained in their early years that "The qualities deemed necessary for adulthood—the capacity for autonomous thinking, clear decision making, and responsible action—are those associated with masculinity and considered undesirable as attributes of the feminine self."[2]

There is the young Randolph Lamm, busying himself with his wife's art gallery, making unilateral decisions about where and how they will live. He is the demanding young artist focused on his writing and his cinema rather than the emotional complexities of his wife and, later, his family. He mentions their trip to Indiana as an aside. For her, it was a response better than suicide based on the shame of an out-of-wedlock child. "I'm amazed it took me so long to get over the idea that a woman was somehow less than a man," Jennifer Lamm says today. But still, she does not travel because Randolph will not or cannot. Her life—then and now—is locked in his world's orbit. Then and now, she seeks a place for herself within their world.

"These stereotypes reflect a conception of adulthood that is itself out of balance," Gilligan continues, "favoring the separateness of the individual self over connection to others, and leaning more towards an autonomous life of work than towards the interdependence of love and care."

The "splitting of love and work" occurs in the separate but linked narratives of the Lamms. Mr. Lamm details a work history, a progression of jobs taken and lost, of projects (the film society, photographing) engaged and then completed. There was a "period of great talk" coinciding with his period of great work. Now, in retirement, silence is the complement to no work. With this, he says, he is content. That may be simple posturing (weeks after our meeting his son told me that Mr. Lamm talked with pride about our interview), but it represents how he sees himself. It is not, however, how Jennifer Lamm sees him or herself.

A key to her narrative is, I think, her fear of becoming a "thing," an object of professional ministration or familial obligation. In remembering the elder German woman for whom she once cared, a woman to whom she ministered because the daughter was too busy, she says with horror that "they were treating her like a thing!" To be a dependent object rather than an independent (or interdependent) being, to be cared for rather than to care for another—that is Mrs. Lamm's greatest fear, a fate literally worse than death. At the same time, the failure of her and Randolph's relations with both children and grandchildren deprives her of the intimacies she needs.

"Control is what it is all about," she says. But the tension between independence and interdependence is the crux of her story. In parenting and in her world, dependence is what children grow out of, what adults in maturity leave behind. That was the lesson of her generation and one that now haunts her. Adult women cared for their children, controlled the family. And now, without that relation—and without an adult interdependence—she is in danger of becoming a "thing," an object for care. The relation with a husband is not enough.

Her need is not simply for Randolph's presence but for their children's involvement. More generally, it is for a social context—"Now, we see no one. My social life is up there at the Y"—limited by her hearing deficit and their physical isolation. And so she tries to involve husband, children, and sometimes friends in her plans for voluntary euthanasia, to make her death simultaneously an act of not only independence (*my* death!) but of interdependence. It was the fear of familial and social estrangement that caused her to contemplate suicide at the time of her first pregnancy. Now it is a need for familial involvement that sends her to her sons and her husband, seeking control of death—a date, a method of expedition—as a way of involving them in her life. She wants their support, their assistance, and if she is a bother at least they can help her die. From Randolph she seeks a death pact with a cutoff date that they can agree on—together.

"Euthanasia shares this feature with intense individualism: it is a very powerful expression of seeking control," writes McGill's Margaret Sommerville.[3] It is not simply that those who are dying "most need a sense of personal identity," but that for some, and I think Jennifer Lamm is among them, advocacy and preparation for euthanasia represent a way of asserting control and individualism in a context where they feel alienated and alone.

"Burden is a word I hate," she says, and it is here that the issue of feminism and a woman's relation to others becomes so critical. As a woman who "just gave up everything. I put myself in Randolph's hands," she *was*, for years, a dependent adult. He brought her records to listen to, topics for articles he wanted her to write. He criticized her and her sister's art gallery. As a full-time parent she was in charge of the lives of dependent children who now, in maturity, are independent of her and simultaneously distant, either geographically or, with David, in terms of perceived involvement in her life.

Exacerbating this, she is like many who are hearing impaired, distanced by an infirmity that inhibits intimacy and normal relations. Gossip and chatter among the women in her swimming group pass her by. Her grandson mumbles inaudibly, thus providing another impediment to her relation with him. Telephone calls from her family in Buffalo are hard to hear. It is a signal aspect of hearing impairment that even among those one loves, the person feels alone. Misunderstood words, fragments of sentences when thoughts are offered, are insufficient to feel the community of another's thoughts. In addition, however, there is here the isolation of having moved from one city to another, from a place of familial history—Buffalo—to one where they knew almost nobody. Leaving Buffalo and the once close-knit relationship with her daughter-in-law, Susan, Jennifer Lamm has entered, in Durham, a new relationship not with a son she perceives as too busy, too distant, but again with a daughter-in-law, Christine, who becomes the one best friend.

And so for Jennifer but not Randolph Lamm, life remains unresolved, a work in progress. She looks forward if he does not. Her freedom from responsibility for their children is balanced by sadness at the lack of that responsibility. The need to do nothing is challenged by a feeling that there should be more to do—that these years should be full in a way, perhaps, that they are not. There is a private anger, perhaps years in the making, against those elements of her and Randolph's life that led to the familial rupture, a sense of missed opportunities (for travel, for relations with her siblings, for what she gave up in her marriage) that is still unresolved, still affecting her present but not his.

NOTES

1. From the poem "Under Ben Bulben," Yeats' epitaph: "Cast a cold eye on life, on death. Horseman, pass by!" See M. L. Rosenthal, ed., *Selected Poems and Two Plays of William Butler Yeats* (New York: Collier Books, 1962), 190–193.

2. Carol Gilligan, *In a Different Voice: Psychology Theory and Women's Development* (Cambridge: Harvard University Press, 1982), 17.

3. Margaret Somerville, Euthanasia by Confusion, *UNSW Law Journal* 20, no. 3 (1997): 1–20.

11

The Millennium Watcher

Being over seventy is like being engaged in a war.
All our friends are going or gone and we survive
Amongst the dead and the dying as on a battlefield.
                    Muriel Spark (*Momento Mori*, 1959)

Mrs. Bee is an exception. At the time of her interview she was battling a metastatic cancer whose spread had disabled the arm and shoulder where, forty years before, she had undergone a radical mastectomy. Her prognosis was poor and, indeed, she died within a year of this interview. Unlike the other narrators, therefore, she was in the early stages of a terminal illness that, irrespective of age, creates a perspective with unique social and psychological characteristics.

But Mrs. Bee wanted to talk, wanted me to understand what her life was like at this point. And because of my affection for her, I taped this interview. It was interrupted by her home aide's demand that she have her dressing changed. We were to continue it when she felt better but, within weeks, she was too sick to pick up the narrative where it was left on that day.

Within this series she holds a particular place. A friend of my parents, she had been particularly close to me during the years I cared for my father, Norm. Her references to him relate her narrative here to my book about his last years, *Mirrored Lives*, adding depth to the story of my father's care from the perspective of his cohorts. As critically, perhaps, her daughter-in-law, Carol, spoke movingly and at length about Mrs. Bee's care in *A Place in Time*.

And so, six years after first transcribing this narrative, I read it again. It is the story of a person with a critical, terminal illness whose perception of that condition is affected by her perception of age. Despite—or perhaps because of—the associations with previous stories and my own personal history, it seemed a fitting narrative fragment with which to end this section.

I won't say life's sweet, but I'm not ready to die. I'm still fighting. I do fight. I have to see the new century. I don't know why. I'm sure it's not going to be any different. But sure, why not? It would be nice to see my eleven-year-old granddaughter Sara married, but I haven't told her that! I don't want to hasten that day. No, I'm not ready to give up. I mean, sometimes it never gets beyond the drag of it, but I'm always hopeful. I can't imagine giving up at this point. I can't imagine the situation where I would say, "I'm going to turn my face to the wall and I don't want to wake up." I'm not ready to give up. I wish we could make our life a little more interesting, a little less routine.

Routine is so difficult. We never get beyond it. Some of that is in our thinking. Some of that is actuality, I'm sure. Mostly I've just kept busy doing what had to be done, my whole life. Today I get up and, with help, it's twelve o'clock before I'm dressed and have my exercises done. If I want to button my own blouse, it takes ten or fifteen minutes because of my bad arm. But if someone else does it for me—it's done. You saw me trying to get a plate down from the shelf. Putting out a plate for you, impressing you. "Have a piece of fruit!" Alone, I would just eat with my fingers!

It really is a switch, and my mind just isn't there yet. It's terribly frustrating. Like going to the market. I can drive to the supermarket, but I can't reach the things on the shelves. Some of the nicest people, people I've smiled at in the supermarket for twenty years—we've no idea of each other's names—and after they've seen me once or twice with the sling on, they realize, "She didn't just fall, and this isn't going to come off." And they will offer to do something for me. They ask, "What's happened to you?" I say I injured a nerve and let it go at that. And then it's, "Oh, let us help you," or "Can I take your cart out to the parking lot for you?" Then I don't mind saying, "Can you reach that for me?" But how many times can you stop someone you've never seen before and say, "Will you hand me that from the top shelf?" Well, you can, maybe, but you don't.

On the other hand, there's a woman I met—and I haven't seen her in ages—who for some reason lost the use of her one arm. And she said she finally got to the point where she could put nail polish on with her teeth!

Now, that's something to aim for. She lives alone, apparently. I don't know if I could live alone.

Part of this is a function of age. It's taking the time I'd like to be spending doing something else, this is the thing. Life gets narrower and narrower. My husband, Ray, likes the quiet life we're leading. He works from nine to four as an investment counselor handling other people's money and he comes home tired. It's such a dirty trick to him. When we were talking about insurance, I used to say, "Well, I'll always be there to take care of you. And if I think you need nurses, you'll have them." But the person we have to worry about is me, because after all I'm six years younger. I was to take care of him. Well, all of a sudden, this has gone topsy-turvy. We don't talk about it. He doesn't want to make any plans. We'll manage, period. Do I want him to talk about it? Sure. After all, you have to know which way you're going, what's important and what's not important. But that's not Ray.

Some of my friends have said that my mind hasn't adjusted to the stage my body has gotten to. I mean, I'm still thinking of myself as able to do things that I can't do. I can't do things on my own schedule. Well, you know, for example, at a few minutes past four o'clock, I'll have to say to you, "Excuse me, I have to go change my sleeve." That's it. I can't just say, "Let's talk some more." There are limits placed on me from outside. Well, that's a great change. I can feel myself thinking, "Well, I can do this or I can do that." I need to go to bed at night. I can't stay up and read a book and then get up the next morning. And that's horrible. I mean, I've got to get up the next morning. And it's not just that I can't do it physically. It's that emotionally or mentally or from the standpoint of energy—I don't have that any more. And I can't do it. And my mind hasn't got there.

I'm still thinking, "Well, gee. It would be fun to take a trip." But, you know, I'm not going to take a trip again—unless my daughter-in-law, Carol, goes with me. She helps me here, but I can't ask her to take a trip with me. And neither Ray nor I can lift a suitcase anymore. And you can take the most beautifully guided tour of Europe, but there's a point where your guide does not go with you. You have to go alone. You have to lift your bag. You can't always count on the person in front of you or behind you putting your bag up for Customs to rummage through, so they can see what you're sneaking into the country. [*Laughs.*]

It's funny, in the last few years, there have been the people who were well and the people who were not well. Some people have stayed healthier than others, and until all of this flared up, I was one of the healthy ones. And everybody was doing for everybody. We'd stop and say, "Let's take so-and-so with us," or "Let's take this to so-and-so." And everybody was getting very tired and saying, "I've got to start thinking about myself." I mean, that's a phrase you hear. "I'm doing it for myself," or "I've got to think of me." They'd say, "I meant to go but, oh! I just had all these errands to do, and then by three o'clock I was tired and wanted to go home. I've got to start thinking of myself."

It's horrible. All of a sudden, I've gotten so old. Do you realize that? Now I'm in the other position, I'm in the other chair. It's weird! I can't do as much as I used to. Instead of thinking of myself like you, from your point of view—healthy—I'm over there where your father, Norm, was. There are people in our group who just went to pieces and died quickly. But there aren't many people like this [*points to sling*]. To be handicapped, but not to die, that's the adjustment. I can say it now, though. My handicap shows. I could do without Eleanor [*the day aide*], but I would be spending all my time picking up all the things I dropped. That's an awful life to look forward to.

It's horrible. Absolutely horrible. You no longer trust anybody. You don't know why anything is being said. Is something being said to be nice, to be sweet? What's the other side of the laugh? And, you know, now I'm just one more responsibility. "Well, let's come out and see poor Ruth." Ruth wants to give them a big, fat kick. I don't want to be a responsibility. I'm sure I'm a responsibility to them. "If she stumbles, who is going to pick her up?" I'm sure that's what they're thinking. They don't think of it consciously, but, well, you know. This is what comes through to me. I hadn't ever thought of myself that way. All you have to do is look at me—and here's the sling. I can't cut my bread. I frequently need help getting into and out of a car, or they think I do. They've got to react to it.

I don't mean to be hard on them. I think they care. But I think I'm frightening to them. And Mother was frightening to her friends. As you know, I helped care for her for many years. Her friends would say to me, "I just can't come to see your mother anymore. That's the way I could be." And I think the speed with which this happened to me—I mean, there was no preparation. And I'm the youngest of my friends. I think it's frightening to them. For me, as well, it really is a switch, and my mind just isn't there yet. I'm sure Mother's wasn't all those years ago. It has to be terribly frustrating. You had to put yourself in her place and realize what she wanted to do.

At the same time it was fascinating to me. I can remember Mother, her last birthday or anniversary before [*her second husband*] Walter got too sick to enjoy things like that. We'd all had lunch together, and she'd gotten lobsters in for us. We cooked them and ate them. And then the others left, they had things to do, and she said, "Now don't go, Ruth. We have to clean the shrimp because people will be coming in tonight." Boy, didn't we clean a pound of shrimp! Then nobody came in. But you know, she was still pushing to do the things that belonged to her life. You can't suddenly take it away from her. And then I had to dash home to make supper for my family.

These things don't start overnight. They don't just start one day and everything was fine the day before. I can remember on Walter's eightieth birthday, him saying to his son George, "Something's funny. Mother said we had to go into Dad's bedroom to write the cards." And with that she walked into her bedroom and started clearing out her drawers. It was . . . a bit crazy. You know what I mean. And Walter said, "That was a little lapse." I hadn't realized. And there were other little things like that. Gradually, I was doing more and more for her. I mean, I spent my time there, and if I didn't, she was here. Even so she had nurses, aides around the clock.

Walter died in '67, and Mother died in '74. We already had nurses for Walter in his last year, off and on. She had a stroke just before he died. He was in the hospital dying and she apparently had a slight stroke. And earlier, we had a nurse for a bit, then she fired the nurse. I remember George saying, "You can't get somebody in until she reaches the point where she can't do anything for herself." She had another stroke and needed help, and finally gave up completely. It had to be from '67 to '74.

We'd say to Mother, "Oh, can we do this for you?" or "Can we do that?" I knew that, doing it at her pace, she still was a person who had a right to make up her mind about what was important to her. To me, she was that kind of person. She got to the point of saying at the end, "I've appreciated what you've done for me." But she couldn't say, "I've given you a hell of a time." And there was a point where I suddenly realized this wasn't the person I'd grown up with.

The fact that I have cancer—I haven't even had time to think about it, I'm so busy trying to function. Getting twelve hours of something done in a six-hour day, it seems. I haven't even dealt with that. It hasn't hit yet, which is stupid. "I haven't even cleaned the bureau drawers," I say to myself. Do you know the significance of that? If you're going away, or going to hospital, your drawers should be in order. That's what we were taught, you know. In other words, your life should be in order. You don't know how messy I am.

I haven't really faced up to that yet. I'm too busy coping with the daily routine. Just think: if you want to start a new box of cereal, I don't want to just tear off the flap with my teeth. I want to be able to close that box of cereal. And I want to be able to fold down the plastic inside the box to keep the cereal fresh. Then, to do that, you have to cut it very carefully. Well, you try to do it with one hand! It takes time. And some of those plastic bags inside the boxes tear easily and some don't. And it infuriates me when they're messy. That can take me a good half hour! And there's not that much time in the day. Then I pass certain things off, and leave certain things. But there are certain things you can't leave undone. There comes a point where you and "it" have to face each other.

What medical help I've gotten, I've gotten because I fought for it. At this point, I don't think anyone really thinks it's worth doing. I thought doctors had feet of gold and knees of gold and hearts of gold. It was hard to discover that they didn't. I think they just felt I wasn't worth it. We know there isn't anything to be done except to maintain. I don't think there's any question they think I'm old and not going to improve, and it isn't worth fussing about. You know, "Anything that makes her happy, that makes her more comfortable, is good." And I've had a couple of people say that probably I'm right. I mean, I don't know. I feel I don't really know how to go about these things.

I went from place to place. I've never shopped for doctors before in my life! I wasn't smart enough to know that a heavy arm like mine—heavy because of the mastectomy I had in the 50s—could cause problems.[1] And it had. It had caused a separation at the shoulder. And so I said, "Well, I need to have some help." So they sent me to the area hospital, but I didn't have a doctor there, so nobody was watching me. Then my son said, "I hear there's a great clinic at this other hospital. Why don't you go?" So I did, and they gave me a splint. When I took the splint back to the first hospital, they said, "Humph. That was a good idea. I wonder why we didn't think of that."

Finally I talked to somebody else who said, "There's a nice young doctor who is not going to give you any false hope but will look at you and make suggestions." That was out at the rehabilitation center, which is part of General Taylor Hospital. And he said—and another doctor that I trust said—"You're not going to get better, but you've got to exercise or you're going to lose whatever you have, and it's going to be much more painful." And he gave me the exercises, and said, "We'll work with you for a month. And if you make progress, we'll keep you. If not, we'll make other arrangements for you." Well, there was no progress, but at least I maintained where I was.

The kids were six and three when I had my first mastectomy. How did I get through it? In those days you got better. You went home from the hospital and their way of reacting was to wet the beds every night. So instead of climbing the walls, I hung sheets. I mean, that was just as good as therapy. And I did it because we didn't have a dryer. I was getting better and better, and able to do more and more. With this one, at this time it's stable. I guess.

I never lost the use of my arm. I was doing as much as I ever did, as much as you can do after surgery. My recovery was to all intents and purposes fine. The first time I had a biopsy, I was afraid. Why wouldn't you be? We didn't know much about cancer then.

And the second time I went out for dinner from the hospital—they said you can go out. They really hadn't planned on doing the mastectomy. They thought this was nothing at all. It was "any lump has to be biopsied." Then it was bam! A radical mastectomy. That was the way they did things in those days.

POSTSCRIPT

For two generations the Bee and Koch families have lived in close association. My Aunt Janice and Mrs. Bee were primary school friends; Ruth Bee and her husband were my parents' closest friends. During the years I cared for my father, Mrs. Bee became my confidant, constantly comparing her period of parental caregiving with my own. When she became ill, I spent as much time with her as was possible. During that period she was eager to participate in this project, to help in my work.

Although Mrs. Bee doubted the interest of her physicians in her care—"I think they just felt I wasn't worth it"—I did not. Their bedside attitude may have been minimal, but their efforts, from my perspective, were sincere. It may well be that her personal physician should have recognized the symptoms of her cancer earlier, but a number of treatments were attempted over the course of several years. At one point she was offered a radical operation that would have removed her arm and shoulder but saved her life. After much thought, she declined.

Her insistence on physician disinterest reflected, at least in part, the general sense of social alienation she felt as a result of her disability. "Now I'm in the other position," she said, a care receiver rather than, as she had been across her life, a caregiver. "You no longer trust anybody. You don't know why anything is being said." Feeling herself frail and unworthy, she doubted the concern of others for her. Mrs. Bee did not want to be seen as needy in the way she had seen her friend, my father Norm. To be old and self-reliant, able to help the less fortunate, was for her appropriate. She felt being the person who others felt compelled to visit was demeaning and wholly inappropriate.

It is this as much as the fact of longevity that defined age to her. "All of a sudden, I've gotten so old. Do you realize that? Now I'm in the other position, I'm in the other chair." Age, in short, was defined by her as illness, the inability to do for oneself. Put another way, Mrs. Bee did not see herself as old because she was more than seventy years of age. When she could travel, drive, and care for others as well as herself, the fact of having lived more than seventy years was a datum irrelevant to her life style. For her mother, my father, and now herself: Age was only minimally related to longevity. It was intimately bound up in the fact of a limiting, physical condition.

Nine months after this interview, Mrs. Bee died at home. At her funeral several people of her generation told me how old they felt, how frail they were. This woman's arthritis required a cane. That woman had progressive hearing loss. All equated longevity with disability. All saw in their frailty a continuity, which I perceived as strength. My own visual disabilities were, they said, especially unfortunate in a "young man" in his middle years. I had become, through them, a provisional member of their league.

As I gave a eulogy for Mrs. Bee, I scanned the congregation and saw several cancer survivors and four or five individuals who had in their fifties or sixties had cardiac bypass operations. There was one person in a wheelchair and a few people who needed canes to walk safely. They kept them almost surreptitiously hidden beneath their coats. While praising Mrs. Bee, the person I had known, I noted that in almost any age group there would be nearly this same level of disability. The difference was, however, that while younger persons see their illnesses as an aberration and perhaps a challenge, these people had been trained to assume longevity and frailty were synonymous. In my speech I praised Mrs. Bee for her strength and the manner in which she had cared for us all. I called her longevity a virtue, asking who among us younger people might hope to do as well. Age isn't about disability or disease, I concluded. It is about the mortality we adults all know far too well.

I thought I saw some people nod as I spoke. Afterwards, however, Mrs. Gleeson—a bridge companion of Mrs. Bee's—came by to chat. "You captured her, you know. You made us laugh," she said to me. "But Thomas," she continued, "you don't know a thing about age. Just wait until you're eighty years or so. Then you'll have something to talk about."

NOTE

1. The arm became "heavy" because of fluid buildup following removal of not just the breast but also the lymph nodes on the affected side of her body. It was a condition she had lived with for forty years, and the first symptom of her cancer was an increase in problems on this side of her body.

Discussion: The Experience of Age

At seventy-seven it is time to be in earnest.
Samuel Johnson, *Journey to the Western Isles of Scotland*, 1775

The myths of age simply do not match the individual realities of the lives they purport to describe. How could they? Academics and popular writers alike have constructed a portrait of the elderly at once so general and so contradictory that it includes everybody and nobody at once. As Steven Katz writes, "At one and the same time they [the elderly] are characterized as a financially secure, healthy, homogeneous, powerful interest group, and as a massive, dependent burden on welfare, health programs, and the tax base generated by the currently shrinking workforce. In either case, they are seen as taking a disproportionate share of society's resources and disrupting intergenerational relations in the process."[1]

Neither pole of this rather bipolar summary describes the lives of my co-authors, the narrators of this book. None, for example, are "greedy geezers" spending the inheritance of younger readers on frivolous, self-indulgent travel and toys. Despite the dire warnings of demographers and statisticians, these people will not bankrupt succeeding generations. Alex Sarnoff is neither rich nor dependent on the largesse of his children. Nor is Elizabeth Greer. Although the Hardings are comfortably middle-class citizens, Jake Epp gets by on a minor pension, and, like the Lamms, with Social Security payments that are little more than sufficient. As Jennifer Lamm reminded us all, monies received from Social Security are not gifts but the return of mandated payments invested for decades in a system of income deferral their generation first created and then supported through years of payroll deduction.

And yet, we assume that seniors are not merely profligate but somehow organized in their rapaciousness. Ironically, this is a legacy of the years of Ronald Reagan's geriatric presidency. By 1990, the assumptions of the self-consciously grasping senior class had become so ubiquitous that John L. Hess was moved to write, in *The Nation*, the "confessions of a greedy geezer":

I see by the papers, damn near every day, that I'm a Greedy Geezer. Not any old greedy geezer, either, but one of those quintessentially avaricious members of the breed called Notch Babies, hailed by *The New Republic* in a widely quoted tribute as, "spiteful, singleminded, and, to the uninitiated, deeply baffling—a parody of a special interest group." Another common compliment was rendered by George Will in *Newsweek* this way: "The elderly are not more rapacious than the rest of us, they are just better at being so." The general idea is that we take time from our golf and our yachting to scare the daylights out of politicians.[2]

Rapacious? Tell it to Jake Epp, whose income just covers the costs of his walk-up apartment, food, and beer. Or Randolph Lamm, perhaps, who sits in his great silence, remembering active years. Retired newsman and newsmaker Walter Chronkite is a yachstman, Tim Harding is not. Former U.S. presidents are almost by definition golfers. Alex Sarnoff is not. The only activist in the group is Sherry Busch. If she ever scared anybody—except, perhaps, one of her former husbands—it would be a delightful piece of news to her.

Avaricious and grasping? On the contrary, these people make no grand claim on the community's resources and ask surprisingly little of society at large. Indeed, many exemplify the generous process of intergenerational transfer in which seniors provide monies for the necessities of the younger generation. It is not simply that seniors leave their savings to younger relatives—important a source of wealth as that may be.[3] Far from bankrupting their younger relations, seniors support them across the span of their shared lives. More prosaically, Sherry Busch lends her credit card to a niece who will never repay the money she "borrowed." Holly Treeson hopes to live long enough to pay off her mortgage so her apartment will be available—free and clear—as a legacy for her younger relatives. In this she follows a more general pattern. Seniors are the single most important source for the down payments by young adults buying a first home.

Still, statisticians insist seniors use a "disproportionate share of society's resources," a position that assumes an easy answer to proportionate distribution. There is, however, no generally accepted formula defining a percentage of health and social service budgets that must go to children, adolescents, young adults, and the elderly. This is instead a default assumption, one reached on the basis of reflexive prejudices that have no independent weight. If seniors aren't productive, then, by definition, their use of public resources is unproductive and too costly. It is true that some seniors—Holly Treeson, for example—need and receive extensive care, drawing on public monies set aside for that purpose. So too, of course, do many younger people whose lives are limited by accident or illness.

For most, the "disproportional share of society's resources" that the elderly supposedly grab is based on their need for health care services. Certainly, most of these narrators have ailments requiring treatment from public and private insurers. Some will be like Jake Epp or Elizabeth Greer's husband, Lloyd, dying quickly and without expensive care. Others have private insurance—the Hardings for example, and the Lamms—that gives them health coverage in return for monthly premiums.

Their need as individuals is only "disproportional," however, when compared to that of healthy, younger adults as a class. Among the many existing communities of need, however, it is only those who are both elderly and frail who are condemned on the basis of the expense of their continuance. We do not say the same of those who test positive for the HIV virus, for example, expensive though their treatment may be. Nor does society castigate for his or her disability the infant with cerebral palsy, the adolescent with Duchane's muscular dystrophy, or the middle-aged adult with multiple sclerosis. Although these and other people at risk require expensive, continuing care, none but the fragile senior are castigated for that necessity. The idea of equitable shares based solely on age is itself ageist, reflecting not the strengths and needs of a range of individuals but categories and barriers constructed by social scientists and the statisticians who accept their definitions. And, as Jennifer Lamm points out, the Medicare benefits they receive—like the Social Security checks that sustain them—are the result of an equitable social vision these and other seniors have supported for years through tax payments.

More centrally, the assumption that illness and fragility are necessary characteristics of age is itself incorrect. "The reality is that the forces driving health care costs have little to do with demographics and are largely within our control."[4] The equation—age equals costly, dependent fragility—is a scapegoat; in other words, a way in which blame for systemic failures of the health care system can be assigned easily if not reasonably to a single population.[5] A MacArthur Foundation study by John W. Rowe and Robert L. Kahn, published in 1998, argued that the reverse is true. "Older Americans are generally healthy," it said. "Even in advanced old age, an overwhelming majority of the elderly have little functional disability, and the proportion that is disabled is being whittled away over time."[6]

By focusing on the potential for first illness and then dependence in some near future, we have defined continuance itself as a disease, making of longevity a clear pathology. From Simone de Beauvoir's *Coming of Age*[7] to modern works on the psychology of aging, those surviving past the age of sixty-five or seventy years have been named as necessarily fragile, needy, and diminished. As Stephen Katz notes, it takes only a simple substitution to make the case for constructed age that Foucault argued for sexuality: "[Age] appeared as an extremely unstable pathological field: a surface of re-percussion for other ailments, but also the focus of a specific nosography, that of instincts, tendencies, images, pleasure, and conduct."[8] This has be-come an article of demographic faith, albeit one not necessarily reflected in the lives of these or other individual seniors.

Equating age with illness obscures a central strength of these narrators and their contemporaries. Whatever their current needs or future require-ments, they have been for many decades paragons of health. Their vaunted fragility is offset by a healthy endurance that has given their lives a longev-ity that is remarkable. People who today are past seventy years of age have survived into a seniority in which medicine can treat—medically or surgi-cally—a host of conditions that once decimated the ranks of their contem-poraries. These are, after all, people born to the age of influenza and poliomyelitis epidemics; to widespread death from a host of killing illnesses of yesterday: pneumonia, tuberculosis, and a multitude of cardiac condi-tions. Fragile? Not hardly. One and all, the narrators and their contempo-raries are survivors.

In the same vein, because they do not work these narrators are assumed to be burdensome, a drain on social resources. They are thus assumed to be at best neutral if not in fact negative forces in the social drive for produc-tion. But this may not be their choice. Although there is intense social pressure for the young and the middle aged to advance in their careers, to improve their condition and progress economically, the reverse is true for seniors. They are expected to neither work nor advance themselves in soci-ety. All have had their chance at success, at achievement. To seek it again in their dotage is, in our culture, perceived to be unseemly.

As a class, seniors have been retired by corporate policy and federal laws that mandate their dismissal from the workforce at an age of fifty-five to sixty-five years. "Older men and women are not given an equal chance for paid employment," in the words of one report. "Millions of older people are ready, willing, and able to increase their productivity, paid and voluntary."[9] The question is not their willingness or competence, but in most cases society's adamant insistence that they "make way" for younger and therefore presumably more deserving workers.

Simply, they have been denied on the basis of chronology access to activities within a society in which their strengths and capabilities otherwise would be welcomed and may be needed. Whatever their previous successes, the most seniors can look forward to in the workplace is volunteer work or parttime employ in fast food restaurants. Social scientists call this a "structural lag," the distance between abilities and resources imposed by the social structure itself.[10] It is thus not surprising, perhaps, that they exist on pensions, on money saved. Few other options are open for them.

If they have been barred from the workforce by age or physical limitation, however, it is hardly fair to condemn them for not working. Some are indeed too ill to work, and perhaps too ill to serve a more than minimal role in their communities. Holly Treeson and Jake Epp are two examples. But if we are to dismiss them for this, then we also must banish as expensive and unworthy the thousands of younger people whose infirmities—multiple sclerosis, for example, or ALS, cerebral palsy, psychiatric disorders, and cardiac complaints—cull them, too, from the healthy, working population. Unless we are to condemn equally those populations—and the younger, idle rich who also do not work—then to blame seniors for their leisure is to insist that they pursue what we prohibit, an active place in the economic world.

The fact of enforced unemployment does not mean seniors do not work, of course. As a class they provide volunteer services—unremunerated and thus uncounted by most economists—that are critical. Virtually every public institution in the United States and Canada depends on senior volunteers. They are the people who drive the cars and deliver the food for meals-on-wheels, who serve as assistants in hospitals, docents at zoos and art galleries.[11] Seniors teach remedial reading to children and illiterate adults. They are unpaid baby-sitters for grandchildren and unpaid home carpenters and cooks for their own, adult children. That they are unpaid does not mean seniors are an inconsequential resource.

Similarly, to insist that seniors are "disrupting intergenerational relations" is curious. These aren't interlopers, gate crashers at a private party.

They are one of those intergenerational groups, the elderly parents of aging children with whom they have talked and fought and loved across a life-time. Some have little to do with now middle-aged offspring who have lit-tle to do with them. Others are indeed concerned with children and grandchildren who in their turn are involved with them. But in these lives it is more often the younger and not the elder generation—the children of the Hardings or Jake Epp, for example—who deny shared historical rela-tionships. It is Jennifer Lamm's son, David, who walks so fast his mother cannot keep up, and when asked to slow down, refuses her request.

Others like Sherry Busch are demonstrably caught up in the lives of younger relations who may, for their part, be either supportive or exploi-tive. Many are like Elizabeth Greer, content within their own communi-ties, but still enmeshed in the lives of sometimes distant children whom they visit when it is convenient—or at least not too inconvenient—to their adult off-spring. Mrs. Bee is the exception here, a woman living near a child and grandchildren with whom she is daily involved.

Whatever the interaction, it is the ebb and flow of relationships, the re-sult of lives lived in association. Seniors are no longer the conductors of ei-ther family feuds or familial interaction. If intergenerational relations are "disrupted," the elderly at most share but clearly do not own the blame for that interruption. In some cases, familial and social relations have endured the crises that occur within twenty, thirty, or forty years of involvement. In others, they have not. This is the ongoing fact of intergenerational conflict and resolution played out in every family, whatever the age of its adults. To argue otherwise is to assume that the blame falls only on the most senior person when family fails, when persons become estranged.

POPULAR IMAGES OF AGE

The popular, media-based image of seniors is of a vacuous, demanding, and deeply self-centered congress of eccentric people. It is as if continuance created a personality disorder that deprived the patient of perceptions and social traits younger, more normal people necessarily possess. If the lives of these narrators are any indication, however, that popular portrait of old-sters is caricature based on prejudice—a cartoon image that does not reflect the diverse, complex reality of senior life. There are no *Grumpy Old Men* in this collection. Walter Matthau and Jack Lemmon's scripted silliness is merely a screenwriter's transposition of adolescent rivalries into a retire-ment setting. Randolph Lamm does not spend his days lusting after a younger neighbor; Tim Harding's concerns are more complex and certainly more sophisticated than those of the dipsy elders portrayed by these and other actors. The cantankerously fearful, failing old man crafted with care by Henry Fonda in *On Golden Pond* finds no real-life complement here.

Nor do these female narrators resemble Jessica Tandy—autocratic and out of touch with the changing world—in her role in *Driving Miss Daisy.* Heather Grissom may be physically frail, but she is clearly no out-of-touch biddy uncertain in the face of a changing world. Sherry Busch remains deeply involved in her community and her world. And Holly Treeson, while restricted by illness, is passionately committed to understanding the elements of her life and life history.

"If a young or middle-aged man, when leaving a company, does not recollect where he laid his hat, it is nothing," Sam Johnson once observed. "But if the same inattention is discovered in an old man, people will shrug up their shoulders and say, 'His memory is going.' " Just so. In middle age, a person who forgets a birthday or anniversary, who neglects a social nicety, is preoccupied. We assume that weighty concerns have pushed mundane matters from his or her conscious consideration. Oldsters are expected to be forgetful, however, because we do not expect them to have anything but trivial matters to consider. A parent who is grouchy and irritable is understandably burdened by complex and conflicting responsibilities. The senior who is cantankerous—whatever the reason—is simply an irritating, bothersome old fart. In age, excuses are no longer accepted.

It is hard to separate myth from reality because prejudiced portraits are so pervasive. Having decided there is "gold in gray,"[12] the advertising campaigns of corporations seeking to mine the geriatric market simultaneously present and reinforce an image of seniors unrecognizable in the lived life of these or other elderly citizens I have known. Telephone company advertisements portray seniors as waiting eternally in the living room, hoping for a call from child or grandchild. They have no other lives, these small parables say, except perhaps an intense concern about physical frailties. Martha Raye's mind is focused on the strength of her denture adhesive; June Allison wants to tell the world about the superior quality of adult diapers. Others sell vitamins, Geritol, and medicine for constipation. That's life, the advertisers say, when one has reached threescore and ten years of age.

But if any of this book's narrators has adapted to incontinence—or faces difficulties with their dentures—it is no more a focus of their conversation than baldness, bad breath, or athlete's foot is of mine. It is not that these or other biological concerns are irrelevant, but that they are not sufficiently central to their lives to be made into a topic of our discussions. If constipation troubles any of my co-authors, it is not a problem of sufficient gravity to warrant inclusion in these interviews. It would be remarkable if one's colleague at the office—or a tennis partner at the Racket Club—leaned over and confided the details of his or her constipation, hemorrhoids, or loneliness. Given the closely crafted, public image of seniors gifted to us all by advertisers, it is almost equally remarkable that most seniors share the reticence of younger folk in these areas.

Still, most of my co-authors demonstrate some degree of physical limit that restricts their access to the urban environments in which they live. These they share, however, with a host of us who, while younger, also live with disabilities. Like Jake Epp, I am sufficiently sight impaired to have stopped driving more than a decade ago. With Randolph Lamm, I walk with a limp. Mine results from osteoporosis, however, and his is from other causes. Like Holly Treeson, my middle-aged friends with multiple sclerosis must rely on others to drive them from place to place.

Minor physical failings and chronic, physical limitations are not the exclusive prerogative of age. Whatever our age, we all face the possibility of one or another disability, one or another limit. For these narrators, they are manageable limitations, facts of life rather than barriers to living. "I have so many damn nuisances," Tim Harding says of his Parkinson's and other health problems. "But none of them are going to kill me." This is the attitude narrators like Jake Epp and Holly Treeson take to their chronic infirmities. They recognize the effect one or another disability may have on daily life. But they are not obsessed with bodily functions or their failings. For these people—as for most of us living with chronic physical limitations—a disability is the background against which the central actions of our mundane lives are acted out.

Despite their obvious diversity, these narrators do share with others of their age group some broad physical characteristics. They have reached a point of diminishing bone density, for example, one in which the thickness of the anatomical superstructure is inevitably lessened.[13] And so, Mr. Epp is bandy-legged and thin, all elbows and knees. Elizabeth Greer is round and occasionally resembles—the result of the Meniere's disease and my imagination—a top whose spin is almost ended, gyrating just a bit at the head. They look old, each and every one of them.

Their skin is folded and wrinkled, having lost elasticity, a fact evident to all. "The only thing I get mad at when I look in the mirror is the wrinkles," said Sherry Busch. And, as Elizabeth Greer notes sadly, voices have changed from the strong tenor of maturity to one that sounds—to them and to us, perhaps—tentative and perhaps tenuous. "Somebody taped my voice before," she says ruefully, "and I sounded like an old nag. And I was a lot younger then!"

Certainly, all are at greater risk than their children or grandchildren to the always chancy balance of cell growth and death.[14] But senescence, as the biologists call it—the increasing probability of cellular metastasis or dysfunction with increasing age—is not a matter of immediate reality but of future probability. That any of these narrators might outlive friends and younger relatives is as strong a probability as that one or another will die tomorrow. So what? If we do not discriminate against other populations at risk—younger women with the breast cancer gene, for example—why punish seniors for a greater likelihood of fragility in the nearer future?

CONTINUANCE

Mundanely, these people are distinguished as individuals who have survived at least seventy years in a changing world. As North Americans, they have done so within a common history whose salient features are evident in their conversations. These people were asked about their histories, about what was important in their lives. What they offered in response was personal reminiscence in a context of public events and general histories. This is not a self-centered perspective, however, but a result of the interview process itself. They responded, in short, to my queries. And because all had lived more than six decades of history, each had a lot to report.

"I look at myself and think, boy, the life that's behind me," said Sherry Busch gleefully. "You know, there's not many people who have had the life I've had. I could just sit right down and write the most interesting book." It is a refrain one often hears from those who have survived war, depression, accident, and the illnesses that have claimed less hardy acquaintances across the span of a shared, long life. Holly Treeson describes with extraordinary clarity the transformations of modern medicine that she witnessed as a nurse and now knows as a patient. Tim Harding traveled across the same war theaters that defined Jake Epp's career. Both remember intimate details of World War II, Korea, Southeast Asia.

And while the public history is shared, the experiential knowledge each uses to particularize that history is personal and unique. Elizabeth Greer has not forgotten hard economic times, for example, defined for her by the closing of the bakery where her husband worked. The Depression years for Randolph Lamm were a succession of meaningless, short-term jobs he remembers even now with distaste if not outright rancor. For Heather Grissom, the "Dirty Thirties" were a period of failed businesses and tight money, a time when the resort business died because people had no money for leisure, or even for a plate of fish and chips.

That life has been full and sometimes difficult does not mean, however, that any of them perceive their lives as a finished work. Not hardly. Jake Epp would like to live to be one hundred years old, if only he can do so on his own terms. Mrs. Bee looks longingly at the millennial mark, wondering what it will be like to see this century end and the next begin. Holly Treeson wants to survive at least until 2003, the year when her mortgage will be finally paid off. Jennifer Lamm, a woman afraid of frailty and dependence, tries to convince her husband that they should pick an age when life will be completed so they can commit suicide together. When we reach eighty-five, she says, wouldn't that be grand? Randolph finds the idea indulgent and refuses to engage it.

"Even in the presence of negative factors, and with individual differences taken into account, elderly persons have goals and are open to the future."[15] Why does this surprise us? It says a great deal about ageist assumptions that one must argue that seniors seek a future and possess goals beyond a rapid and, it is hoped, painless death. That the goals and dreams of these narrators are prosaic, their aspirations limited, does not distinguish them from the majority of people whose lives are focused on the necessities of daily existence. It would be nice to think we who are younger strive at important tasks, seeking lofty ends. In the main, we do not. Our lives are spent largely in strenuously mundane endeavors: working to pay the rent, making sure there is food for dinner, hoping for a bit of company and pleasure at the end of the day. Irrespective of age, existence presents for most of us a full course of activity.

AGE AND DEPENDENCE

The signal fear of these narrators is not death but dependence. All are terrified of being unable, of becoming a burden on society and their families. Who isn't? To live a restricted life whose continuance is based on the service of others is a potential no one wishes to experience. "We try to be independent," Holly Treeson says. "*Burden* is a word I hate," Jennifer Lamm insists. Mrs. Bee sees her friends watching her, wondering about her health, and worries that she'll be the next to need assistance in her world. It is a thought that distresses her greatly.

This is not a perspective unique to seniors. Self-reliance, autonomy, and individualism are tenants of the culture at large. The idea of physical dependency requiring care is anathema to most people, irrespective of their age. As the narrator Lucy Day in *Second Chances* points out, learning to accept the assistance of others is difficult for anyone.[16] A model diagnosed with first multiple sclerosis and then breast cancer, she had to learn to see life from the perspective of a wheelchair, to accept help entering or leaving a restaurant or a car. Accepting the limits imposed by her condition was, she suggests, the most difficult part of the condition itself.

Whatever their age, some North Americans would prefer death to physical and social dependency, irrespective of the potential for life's continuance. Heather Grissom may be "ready" to die, but this is not because she's tired of life. She is, however, discouraged by the limits of her physical illness and the dependence that is its necessary companion. The same can be said, however, for many others. Consider the first seventy or so persons who died at the hands of unemployed pathologist Dr. Jack Kevorkian.[17] Most were middle-aged people facing not rapidly terminal but long-term, chronic conditions. Almost all were sufficiently healthy to travel independently to the Pontiac, Michigan, hotel where Kevorkian plied his trade. The average age of those whom he has killed[18] or assisted in suicide is fifty-three years, nine months. Forty-two percent of all his deaths involve adults with Lou Gehrig's disease (ALS) or multiple sclerosis. These are chronic and degenerative, long-term neurologic disorders that require—as a fact of survival—adaptation to physical conditions demanding the patient accept assistance as part of daily life.[19]

What seems to have driven many of these people to Kevorkian's ministrations is a fear of a restricted life—like Lucy Day's, Holly Treeson's, or Tim Harding's—in which physical limitations restrict a full range of independent activity. Physical limits may be feared, but that fear may be surmounted, whatever a person's age, if he or she can accept a life requiring assistance. This was a message of middle-aged fashion editor Jean-Dominique Bauby's 1997 book, *The Diving-Bell and the Butterfly*, which described in intimate detail an emotionally rich if physically "locked-in" existence following a massive stroke.[20] It is also a feature of Stephen Hawking's mystique, and of our admiration for, say, paralyzed actor Christopher Reeve. Disability and physical dependency are not the exclusive prerogatives of age, in short. The challenges of a restricted life can be accepted or rejected at any age. The central issue is disability—not longevity.

A "NATURAL" LIFE SPAN

Within the paradigms of social science, the elderly are defined by their place at the end of the life course or life span. If they're not actively ill, all are still presumed to be terminally afflicted with age. Having "lived out a natural life span," as Daniel Callahan put it,[21] even those who are as active and social as Sherry Busch at best participate in a kind of life's encore; doing one last time what once would have been seen as a real life's work. And yet, a "natural" life span is merely a statistical average, a generalizing number that changes, generation to generation, depending on the science and social reality of each age. Heather Grissom and Sherry Busch's survival are as natural as was the death of Busch's second husband, a man of early middle age. Jennifer and Randolph Lamm's continuance is as normal as that of their children. Neither cellular biologists nor social gerontologists have been able to define with any certainty a "natural" life span, the gift of a specific number of years we are all destined to receive.

The fact that these narrators are nearer the day of their death than the year of their birth is a statistical factoid.[22] What we make of it, however, is social interpretation. "What they have today is all they have," Daniel Callahan assumes. "Even if there is a tomorrow, and a day after that, it will pass all too quickly."[23] That is not, however, how these narrators perceive it. Mrs. Bee wants to live to see her twelve-year-old granddaughter married. Mrs. Greer may have greeted her daughter's announcement of the latter's second marriage with the statement, "Now I can die happy," but she is too involved in her current life to seek a rapid demise. Sherry Busch says she is ready when death takes her, but her schedule is too busy to fit in that visit. She has classes to teach, programs to organize, a buddy system to participate in. Even Jennifer Lamm, who wishes to plan her death, places its occurrence comfortably in the future in a cry for attention that her children and her husband, Randolph, curtly dismiss.

There is no "natural" life span whose years can be named with certainty. Indeed, some researchers believe that within two generations we will all live to be Heather Grissom's age. And yet, because it is assumed these narrators and their contemporaries are preparing to die, they are, some social scientists assume, "disengaging," anticipating their demise by withdrawing from active participation in society at large. Jennifer Lamm is not disengaging, however, even if she is obsessed with control of her death. She reviews her past as a way of changing the relations of her present, with her husband and her world. Sherry Busch is clearly engaged in the activities of her world and those of a range of people, including the seniors she cares for. Jake Epp's life may be restricted by visual impairments, but it is entwined with those of friends, like Lonnie, the reading he would like to do, the Shakespeare he has memorized, and the world of the radio that he listens to with concentration.

With the possible exception of Randolph Lamm, these narrators are not disengaging. They may be detached, however, separated from the rhythms of their mature lives by social and physical factors. They are isolates distanced in a variety of ways from the broader, shared world we younger folks inhabit. They have been retired from social, professional, and familial responsibility. They return to the public arena only occasionally as volunteers—the women handing out orange juice at Red Cross blood banks, the men who serve as commissioners staffing information booths at the train station—or as unpaid child care workers tending the offspring of their own, busy children.

This is not the way they choose to be. Jake Epp still dreams of work, of when he was useful and active. Were it possible, he would like to be out there again. Tim Harding remembers when he was a worthy member of society. The beer steins in his house serve as mnemonics to name the hotels in the cities he visited when he was still an important man. Holly Treeson thinks of her nursing days, of the real work she did when she was both healthy and active. She would do it again if anyone just asked for her help. It is her pride, after all, that she cared for persons who needed her, that her work as a professional counted in the lives of others. Elizabeth Greer misses the days when she worked at the schools, when she was personally important to the then children of her community.

"In American society generally, the values of achievement, productivity, work, progress, and social usefullness accentuate the autonomy and worth of the individual."[24] But these are the very values denied these seniors by chronic disability and the broad segregation of seniors as a class. Even if autonomous, most are seen as less worthy. We assuage or prejudice with the assumption they want it this way, that they are themselves disengaging from the web of professional and personal associations that give meaning to the lives of we who are younger. Instead we have simply assured they would be detached and distanced, floating in a netherworld in which dependence is assumed and the potential of these people to contribute to the common weal is reflexively denied.

Detached from the mainstream of working society, they are also distanced from their communities of history. Supportive families are rare in this group whose children and grandchildren, nieces and nephews, have largely abandoned them. Even in those families in which love and closeness reign—and here Elizabeth Greer's story comes to mind—seniors are often treated as at best extraneous appendages to their children's lives. In some families, history has created its own reasons for intergenerational detachment. Mr. Epp left his children and his wife in Georgia to make the money her treatment and their care required. His children never forgave him. Mr. Harding traveled incessantly and was, when home, no Ozzie and Harriet-style father. And maybe Randolph Lamm was as self-important and autocratic as his and his wife's stories suggest. So what?

It is easy to say, in retrospect, that these men should have behaved differently, of course. But judging the decisions made in a different age is always chancy. Mr. Epp faced the devil's bargain: leave home to support a family or stay at home and assure their poverty. Mr. Harding found a way to feed his family and serve his country that made him an absentee father. If either had stayed home and earned a minimal salary, their children might now condemn them for their failure to provide the foundation of the lives they now enjoy.

THE "LIFE CYCLE"

Believing in a "natural" life span and a "natural" life course, social scientists generally assume seniors, by definition, face similar issues. It is, they say, the inevitable result of the "life cycle" they are completing. Erik Erikson first popularized this view in the 1950s with his book, *Identity and the Life Cycle*.[25] He argued that there is a necessarily progressive, psychological, and social pattern to a "normal" independent life, one that advances from dependent childhood to independent adulthood before lapsing into dependent age. Each stage of life has its essential issues and defining conflicts that build on each other until those who survive face the last stage, the necessary last stage that is old age.

Infancy demands that one learn trust, have hope, and confront in early childhood the idea and ideal of autonomy and individual will. Preschoolers learn initiative while developing a sense of guilt. They gain a sense of purpose that prepares them for early school years in which industry comes with growing competence, defeating the inertia of underachievement. Finally, identity and then intimacy are developed, competence and fidelity their handmaidens, until in nongeriatric adulthood one is productive and "generative" in one's concern for others. Old age somehow reverses the climb to "generativity" and productivity. This last stage is supposedly introspective and individualized, defined by a life review ideally resulting in a "sense of coherence and wholeness" and by "wisdom."[26] That wisdom is the preparation for life's ending, a way to face not life but death with equanimity. Disengagement theory almost inevitably followed from this perspective.

Erikson: Life's Progressive Stages

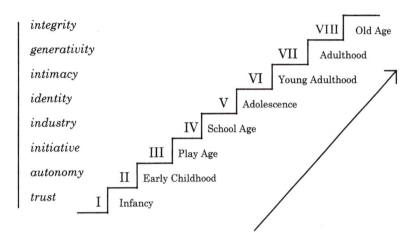

Source: Adapted from Erik Erikson, 1982.

We believe in destinations. "One step at a time," we say, as if life were an amble whose progress and direction can be clearly mapped. "Stay the course," we urge, as if all life requires is that we follow directions like an automobile rally driver navigating a clearly marked course. And so we have assigned a series of stages to life, each with its specific puzzle, each a preparation for the next. The destination is old age and its supposedly unique confrontations. Start with trust and then find autonomy; after that, search for initiative and then industry. Find them and one can locate intimacy, and hopefully, generativity. The route ends with the search for old age's integrity, for wisdom at the end of things. Steady as she goes.

It is life on the ladder, a step-by-step view of an individual's necessarily progressive social development, programmed conflicts at every level, each inevitably and necessarily leading to the next stage. It is like a sixth-grade teacher's lesson plan, a linked and necessary topical advance within a clearly defined time frame. Here, however, the end is not knowing the provincial capitals of Canada or the names of the major U.S. waterways. Rather, the unique and final subject is an old age whose characteristics are assumed to be radically different and unique. Thus, Erikson says, "In old age, all qualities of the past assume new values that we may well study in their own right and not just in their antecedents."[27]

Tell that to Holly Treeson. "I think we should give some thought to educating people that old age doesn't mean you don't have the same desires," she says in rebuttal, "[that] you don't have the same needs—which I suppose is the same thing—that you had when you were much younger." That the emotional and social needs of older people are ones all people share is what gives their stories such poignancy. Like us, they struggle with isolation and the exigencies of community, seek independence while fighting for identity.

Seniors and juniors alike want to participate, but too often find themselves marginalized from the society at large, one seniors themselves helped to create. Indeed, perhaps we dislike them *because* they share our needs, not because they are different. Their lives say to us that issues do not die, fears are not necessarily resolved, battles once fought for independence, autonomy, or productivity are not spoils of war secured forever once they're won. While we live, each presents a concern to which each of us necessarily returns, sooner or later, if we are fortunate enough to survive.

The integrity Erikson reserves for seniors is a sense of "*coherence and wholeness* that is, no doubt, at supreme risk under such terminal conditions as include a loss of linkage ."[28] Because they have been detached by physical or social circumstance from the lives they once led, many of these narrators are indeed unlinked. But this is neither necessary nor inevitable. These values are, for example, elements in the struggle described by non-geriatric narrators in both *Second Chances*, which detailed the patterns of middle-age crisis, and by the caregivers whose narratives are recorded in *A Place in Time*.[29] A loss of linkage is a reality known by people of every age who are distanced by social or physical dysfunction from both personal history—life as it has been lived—and the community in which they have lived it.

It is not life's ladder-like stages, but the protocols of grieving and loss that define the emotional status of both these seniors and of other people learning to live with limits. Elisabeth Kübler-Ross,[30] not Erik Erikson, is the writer whose general paradigm holds sway in these cases. All these narrators are at different stages of grieving, adjusting to the missing pieces of the world they knew, the lives they have lived. Some are in denial, refusing to accept the limits physical or social conditions have imposed on activities and associations they cherished. Others are angry at the losses they as individuals have endured.

The fortunate have, like Mr. Epp and Sherry Busch, come to a point of acceptance, of equanimity in which they can balance what was and what is, then and now in their lives. This is true, however, of all those who face the physical limits of chronic illness. For them, physical dependence need not be a barrier to productivity or intimacy. Independence becomes instead a dispensable luxury and not a necessary virtue of adulthood. Autonomy is transformed into a restrictive assumption, not a physical fact.

The result may be a type of wisdom many assume will be the signal contribution of seniors to the community at large. If so, however, it is wisdom of a peculiar sort. None of these narrators demonstrates an encyclopedic knowledge or an enlightened self-awareness. Certainly Alex Sarnoff does not qualify. Nor does Jake Epp, whose answer to the issues of his world is to light a cigarette and open another can of beer. Mrs. Bee is not calmly self-aware. She is frightened of her condition, withdrawing from her circle of friends because she believes they pity her.

The wisdom they possess resides within their will to endure and the ability to continue to fight the battles of life that continuance requires of us all. It is not that seniors have one battle left to fight in old age. Rather, they must again fight battles first met in childhood and adolescence and perhaps middle age. One may dismiss Erikson's ladder of age while embracing the complex of fundamental, existential issues that he defined as problems to be faced at any age. Each of these narrators revisits one or more of the fundamental struggles as they come to grips with their current lives. Mrs. Bee wrestles with the issue of autonomy, with being dependent rather than being the independently able, giving person. So, too, does Jennifer Lamm, who has struggled with issues of independence and dependence across her forty years of marriage. Mr. Harding ponders the problem of intimacy reflected in his and his children's estrangement. Mr. Epp has lost the remarkable initiative he once possessed. For her part, Holly Treeson fights for the identity that is supposedly the legacy of adolescence.

I do not doubt that we first encounter these lessons one by one. But if autonomy is an ideal first introduced in early childhood, it is also a value that must be reinterpreted again and again across an extended life. Identity is a principal concern of adolescents who seek a way to be in a world they share with parents and contemporaries whose perspective is very different. But crises of identity may occur throughout adulthood when the activities that we choose to define us are challenged. *Second Chance*'s Lucy Days, a fashion model with first multiple sclerosis and then breast cancer, faced it as surely as did Holly Treeson in her fragile years. "Who I am" in relation to a spouse or a family was as much a crisis for that book's character, Richard Wilder—whose wife left him for another woman—as it is for any of the seniors in this book. "I looked in the mirror and nobody was there," he said. "Nobody looked back at me."

In the same vein, the search for comfortable intimacy is not the exclusive prerogative of any single age. Holly Treeson's poignant lament, "I want to share my thoughts, but nobody wants to listen," could as easily be the statement of a teenager as of a physically restricted senior. Elizabeth Greer's affecting description—"I talk to the walls in the apartment now"—of a solitary life in a small apartment is something one might hear from any newly single person without emotional or social support. Intimacy is not a commodity to be secured but an ever-changing posture assumed in relation to others. It is adjusted, day by day and year by year, as the social world we inhabit changes in character and circumstance. The intimacy of a successful, teenage association is not suitable, necessarily, to the necessities of an adult's shared life. We change with circumstance, and the shared world changes with us. And so, as adults, we face the issues of adolescence and childhood once again.

There are some whose ability to relate to others was perhaps always deficient. Tim Harding's "peculiar humor" and the combination—to my mind less than enviable—of an accountant's perspective folded into a military career does not suggest a warm and easily lovable demeanor. And so in old age he must revisit the issue of his relations to his children, and to others, or refuse the battle entirely. In this he has failed and thus is sustained by a single, essential relationship with his wife, Tina. One can, of course, like Randolph Lamm, deny the problem entirely and accept as a virtue the great silence of retirement and modest physical restrictions, taking each day as an existential exercise in meaningless if occasionally pleasant continuation.

The one lesson none of these narrators want to face again is that of elemental trust. They do not readily accept the idea of another's ministrations. All would rather be caregiver than care receiver. "I don't like to think of being in a hospital and being in a wheelchair," Elizabeth Greer says. Who does? But whether one is fifteen or seventy-five, to survive a physically restricted life demands a trust in the care of others that neither age nor experience prepare us to accept. Indeed, the reverse seems to be true. The older we become the less able we may be to accept that diminished physical autonomy does not reduce our potential for identity, intimacy, or initiative.

"They're very much afraid of being hurt," Sherry Busch says of her more fragile friends. "They're so afraid of being handicapped, more than what they are." And if they're not afraid for themselves, their concern is for those persons they love. "It's hard to watch someone who was so independent become dependent," Tina Harding says of her husband. And yet, when was he independent? Not when she worked to help put him through school. Not when she handled his home finances, purchased their homes, and raised their children. He was always dependent on her except in the narrow venue of work, in that one area of his professional identity. Similarly, Mr. Epp wishes to live to become a centenarian if he can do so in his own home and in an "independent" fashion. Of course, his continuance is dependent on the assistance of his friend, Lonnie, and neighbors like me who would visit and assist when required.

Nor is this a singularly male point of view. Holly Treeson is wounded when a neighbor suggests she is dependent on social assistance, wasting public monies through physician home visits. Mrs. Bee is more fearful of dependency, of being the one visited rather than the visitor, than she is of the cancer that affects and finally ends her life. The women no less than the men of this volume value self-sufficiency as a primary virtue second only to the potential for social and interpersonal activity. And yet within the frame of that desired independence, all their lives have been spent interdependently in every way. So too, for that matter, are the lives of we who, while younger, share our seniors' dreams as well as, perhaps, their deficits.

CONCLUSIONS

Narratives and the experiential record are better suited as tools to critique formal theories than as mechanisms for their generation. To build a theory on the fragmentary life histories of a disparate collection of individuals would be as foolish as it has been for others to construct theirs on the shifting ground of social preconceptions and their own inexperience in a long life's trials. Still, on the basis of these lives, and those in other collections, one can advance the following summation.

Old age presents a series of physical characteristics that allow us to visually identify one or another person we would call "old." Oldsters share the fact of continuance, and thus a body of cultural experience and underlying social values that affect not only our view of them but their definitions of themselves. Because they are older representatives of a species whose life span is finite, the certainty is that any person of age will live fewer years in the future than they have in the past.

If they are perceived as a burden, however, it is because we have so defined them. As important, perhaps, it is also because they have accepted a series of assumptions that permits them to be so defined. There is nothing necessarily burdensome about a constituency whose members have lived forty-five, sixty-five, or eighty years. If, however, they are restricted in employment, denigrated in popular tales, and their counsels are reflexively dismissed, it is quite likely few will rise above such discriminatory social barriers. To refuse them social benefits so that younger people can reap more support makes no more sense than to expect adolescents to forego general opportunities so that newborn infants may receive better care.

To the extent we speak of the elderly as frail, we must see them as we do anyone who is disabled by infirmity. If a person has left-side aphasia and paralysis following a stroke, it is irrelevant if that person is thirty-five or seventy-five years of age. Young adult or retiree, that person will require rehabilitation, mobility devices, social and familial support. At present, we designate the younger as worthy of care and the elder simply as old, as if the latter's need was less because he or she had lived longer, and perhaps too long. A lesson of these lives is that seniors feel and worry and think and struggle for their place in our shared community in much the same manner as we who are their younger selves. Each has his or her measure of foolishness, his or her collection of prejudices and deceptions. But in this, too, they are no different from us.

Age is not the last step on some chronological ladder whose rungs are individual and unique. There is no necessary progression of stages we pass through in our lives as if we were ships traversing a canal separating two lakes or two oceans. This is because a conscious life is not a single-track, one-way course whose path is clearly and irrevocably defined. Rather, there are a series of issues, challenges, or problems—call them what you will—that define the human condition in our culture and time. One may confront them first in childhood or adolescence, but each is revisited time and again in need and across maturity. Autonomy and individuality are social values as well as psychological states, culturally defined and socially applied. Trust and intimacy are characteristics defined in association with others, not the result of individual acts of will. Thus, they are challenged whenever our social context is changed, when our place in the shared world is challenged.

Throughout a person's life, the goals of intimacy and social productivity are open for review and redefinition. Divorce or illness may shatter the connections forged over years whether one is thirty years or seventy-five years of age. These are, by definition, events reflecting an ending, although not necessarily termination. Any of these values may thus be challenged two, three, or four times in any person's life. None are the sole prerogative of any human stage of growth because existence is not a course with hurdles set on it for us to run in a certain way. Rather, it is like a shallow lake dotted with reefs and shoals. In passing across or around the lake, one may run afoul of one or more of these hazards two, three, or more times in a life. One learns from the experience, we hope, charts the dangers and their avoidance. If not, well, sooner or later the vessel sinks after being destroyed on them. We call it suicide and it happens to people of every age—especially to teenagers—who find the shared world uninhabitable.

In our society, seniors have come to symbolize not the glories of a long passage but the dangers of the journey itself. And so we represent them as foolish, cantankerous, and demanding folk. We deny them a place in our working society and then condemn them for inactivity. Insisting that they be wiser than others, we castigate those who while not wise are typically no sillier than are we who are their younger selves. Insisting on family as society's integral building block, we take the oldest members of that unit and segregate them in homes for the aged where they can be maintained—ideally at minimal expense—at a distance. It does not have to be this way, of course. That's just how it is. And we do this, if these narrators are to be believed, with the complicity of the seniors themselves. After all, they were our tutors.

There is one signal advantage to longevity that we who are not yet senior do not have. Simply, it is memory. The long stories of these narrators stretch across most of a century. Each remembers care and kindness, success and failure. Seniors can employ a store of experience in confronting their fears and crises. And so, seniority itself—the adaptive lessons of a long life in progress—may support their efforts in a way not available to all. They have been us and thus understand our limits and our fears. Each remembers his or her early, striving years and the indignities they involved. They have not forgotten the issues of being a harried young parent of infants, or of impatient adolescents who wish to be adults. They've progressed professionally in a way that we who are their juniors now seek to engage. They've done these things and understand our limits because they are barriers each of these narrators has him or herself lived with.

We do not like the elderly because they are us, the people we learned from and, if we are fortunate, the people we will someday be. They promoted productivity, demanded respect, and insisted on familial rank ("I'm your father! Do what I say." Or, of course, "I'm your mother, listen to me.") or social position as a definition of maturity. Now they have the temerity to continue in a world they helped make, one in which they seem content to live without clear economic purpose or social stature. And so to us the essential attribute of their world is history, what has been. Their very presence thus reminds us of both past battles and of the frailty of the mortal existence we share.

In the end, it is not the elderly we dislike but our own, mortal selves. At every point in our life we struggle with life's values. We fight for intimacies, battle with autonomy. Each of us seeks a constancy of identity, a permanent posture before the world. Because who we are is defined in relation to the world we share, however, that identity necessarily changes according to

circumstance. We all want wisdom, an understanding of the human condition as each of us experiences it, and are angry with those we would like to
think have its secret. Why can't they tell us? Why won't they make our
pain go away? And if they are foolish, well: how dare they? Shouldn't they
be the ones who hold the salve our lives require, the answers to secrets we
must solve if we are to endure?

In our fear, we have made of seniors a metaphor for all that is tentative
and uncertain in our shared, transient, ephemeral world. Perversely, they
are also the ones who hold in trust our own hopes for an extended future.
They are first and foremost the ones who endured, after all. To be old means
to have learned the trick of survival. Seniors have the perspective that we
who are younger must acquire if we are to get through our own, complex
days. And when they eventually die, we learn from them a lesson that must
be learned again and again by each generation of our species: how to face
mortality. And so we will study them to learn their secret, we will visit on
Thanksgiving and accept their largess at Christmas, hoping for a clue to the
perspective they've obtained. But out of fear and loathing for mortality, we
will not acknowledge them as our own, as extended versions of us all. Why
should we? It's the truth and wisdom most seniors will not acknowledge
themselves because they, too, possess these fears in full measure. It is from
them that we first learned them.

NOTES

1. Stephen Katz, *Disciplining Old Age: The Formation of Gerontological Knowledge* (Charlottesville: University Press of Virginia, 1996), 6.

2. John L. Hess, Social Security Wars: Confessions of a Greedy Geezer, *The
Nation* 250 no. 13 (1990): 437–443.

3. An excellent example of the role seniors play in intergenerational financial transfers is offered by Elizabeth A. Binney and Carroll L. Estes, The Retreat
of the State and Its Transfer of Responsibility, *International Journal of the Health
Sciences* 18, no. 1 (1988): 83–96.

4. Morris L. Barer, Robert G. Evans, and Clyde Hertzman, Avalanche or
Glacier?: Health Care and the Demographic Rhetoric. *Canadian Journal of Aging*
14, no. 2 (1995): 195.

5. Elizabeth A. Binney and Carroll L. Estes, The Retreat of the State and Its
Transfer of Responsibility, *International Journal of the Health Sciences* 19, no. 1
(1988): 83–96.

6. John W. Rowe and Robert L. Kahn, *Successful Aging* (New York: Pantheon, 1998). Also see, "How We Live Determines How We Age." *USA Today*,
March 19, 1998, 80.

7. Simone de Beauvoir, *The Coming of Age* (New York: Putnam, 1972).

8. Michel Foucault, *The History of Sexuality Vol.1. An Introduction.* Translator, Robert Hurley (New York: Vintage Books, 1980), 67. Quoted in Stephen Katz, *Disciplining Old Age*, 7.

9. John W. Rowe and Robert L. Kahn, op. cit.

10. Matilda W. Rile, Robert L. Kahn, and Anne Foner, Eds., *Age and Structural Lag: Society's Failure to Provide Meaningful Opportunities in Work, Family, and Leisure* (New York: John Wiley & Sons, 1994).

11. For an example of the importance of this type of labor to seniors themselves, see Tom Koch, *Mirrored Lives: Aging Children and Elderly Parents* (New York: Praeger, 1990).

12. Meredith Minkler and Anne Robertson, The Ideology of "Age/Race" Wars: Deconstructing a Social Problem, *Aging and Society* 11, no. 1 (1991): 1–22.

13. Robert G. McCulloch, Bone Measurement, Physical Activity, and the Aging Skeleton, *Canadian Journal on Aging* 15, no. 1 (1996): 54–64.

14. A. Comfort, *The Biology of Senescence* (New York: Rinehart Publishers, 1956). Quoted in Karl T. Riabowol, Editorial: Basic Biological Aging Research in Canada: Time for Rejuvenation? *Canadian Journal on Aging* 15, no. 1 (1996): 1–4.

15. Lèandre Buffered, Extension Temporelle des Buts et Âge Chronologique au Cours de la Vieilesse, *Canadian Journal of Aging* 10, no. 3 (1991): 271–288.

16. Tom Koch, *Second Chances: Crisis and Renewal in Our Everyday Lives.* (Toronto: turnerbooks, 1998). Originally published as *Watersheds: Stories of Crisis and Renewal in Our Everyday Life* (Toronto: Lester Publishing, 1994).

17. Tom Koch, On the subject(s) of Jack Kevorkian. *Cambridge Quarterly of Healthcare Ethics* 7, no. 4 (1998): 436–441.

18. A number of these deaths are listed as homicides—that is, they represent a death imposed by another rather than a suicide in which the person is presumed to have participated physically in his or her own demise.

19. For a discussion of adaptive strategies to limiting conditions see, for example, Jenny M. Young and Paule McNicoll, Positive Life Experiences of People with Advanced ALS, *Health and Social Work* 23, no. 1 (1998): 35–43.

20. Jean-Dominique Bauby, *The Diving-Bell and the Butterfly*, Translator, Robert Laffont (London: The Fourth Estate, 1997).

21. Daniel Callahan, *Setting Limits: Medical Goals in an Aging Society* (New York: Simon and Schuster, 1987), 171.

22. That seniors are nearer the day of their death than of their birth is, of course, something that can be said for all of us—including, of course, Daniel Callahan and Richard Lamm—who have passed our thirty-eighth year.

23. Daniel Callahan, op. cit., 42.

24. Sharon R. Kaufman, *The Ageless Self: Sources of Meaning in Late Life* (New York: Penguin, 1987), 123–124.

25. Erik H. Erikson, *Identity and the Life Cycle* (New York: W.W. Norton, 1980).

26. Erik H. Erikson, *The Life Cycle Completed* (New York: W. W. Norton, 1982), 64.

27. Ibid., 64.

28. Ibid.

29. Tom Koch, *A Place in Time: Care Givers for Their Elderly* (New York: Praeger, 1993).

30. Elisabeth Kübler-Ross, *Living with Death and Dying* (New York: Macmillan, 1988).

Bibliography

Barash, David P. (1983) *Aging: An Exploration.* Seattle: University of Washington Press.

Barer, Morris L., Robert G. Evans, and Clyde Hertzman. Avalanche or Glacier?: Health Care and the Demographic Rhetoric. *Canadian Journal of Aging* 14, no. 2 (1995): 193–224.

Bass, Eric B., Stacy Willis, and Ingrid U. Scott. Preference Values in Visual States in Patients Planning to Undergo Cataract Surgery. *Medical Decision Making* 17 (1997): 324–330.

Bauby, Jean-Dominique. (1997) *The Diving-Bell and the Butterfly.* Trans. Robert Laffont. London: The Fourth Estate.

Beauvoir, Simone de. (1972) *The Coming of Age.* New York: Putnam and Sons.

Beauvoir, Simone de. (1984) *Adieux: A Farewell to Sartre.* Trans. Patrick O'Brian. New York: Penguin. Quoted in Kathleen Woodward, *Aging and Its Discontents.*

Binney, Elizabeth A. and Carroll L. Estes. The Retreat of the State and Its Transfer of Responsibility. *International Journal of the Health Sciences* 19, no. 1 (1988): 83–96.

Buffered, Lèandre. Extension Temporelle des Buts et Âge Chronologique au Cours de la Vieilesse. *Canadian Journal of Aging* 10, no. 3 (1991): 271–288.

Callahan, Daniel. (1987) *Setting Limits: Medical Goals in an Aging Society.* New York: Simon and Schuster.

Coles, Robert. (1976) Work and Self-respect. *Daedalus* 105 (1976): 37.

Comfort, A. (1956) *The Biology of Senescence*. New York: Rinehart Publishers, 1956. Quoted in, Karl T. Riabowol, Editorial: Basic Biological Aging Research in Canada: Time for Rejuvenation. *Canadian Journal of Aging* 15, no. 1 (1996): 1–4.

Erikson, Erik H. (1980) *Identity and the Life Cycle*. Second ed. New York: W. W. Norton.

Erikson, Erik H. (1982) *The Life Cycle Completed*. New York: W. W. Norton.

Fisher, M.F.K. *Sister Age*. New York: Vintage Books, 1984.

Foucault, Michel. (1980) *The History of Sexuality Vol.1. An Introduction*. Trans. Robert Hurley. New York: Vintage Books. Quoted in Katz, Stephen, *Disciplining Old Age*.

Gilligan, Carol. (1982) *In a Different Voice: Psychology Theory and Women's Development*. Cambridge: Harvard University Press.

Gubrium, Jaber F. Voice, Context, and Narrative in Aging Research. *Canadian Journal of Aging* 14, no. 1 (1995): 68–81.

Haraven, Tamara K. The Last Stage: Historical Adulthood and Old Age. *Daedalus* 105 (1976): 14.

Heller, Joseph. (1989) *God Knows*. New York: Dell. Reprinted New York: Scribners, 1997.

Hess, John L. Social Security Wars: Confessions of a Greedy Geezer. *The Nation* 250, no. 13 (1990): 437–443.

Johnson, Samuel and James Boswell. (1996) *A Journey to the Hebrides: A Journey to the Western Islands of Scotland & the Journal of a Tour to the Hebrides*. New York: Viking Press/Penguin Classics.

Katz, Stephen. (1996) *Disciplining Old Age: The Formation of Gerontological Knowledge*. Charlottesville: University Press of Virginia.

Kaufman, Sharon R. (1987) *The Ageless Self: Sources of Meaning in Late Life*. New York: Penguin. 123–124.

Koch, Tom. (1990) *Mirrored Lives: Aging Children and Elderly Parents*. Westport, CT: Praeger.

Koch, Tom. (1993) *A Place in Time: Care Givers for Their Elderly*. New York: Praeger.

Koch, Tom. (1998) *Second Chances: Crisis and Renewal in Our Everyday Lives*. Toronto: turnerbooks. Originally published as: *Watersheds: Stories of Crisis and Renewal in Our Everyday Life*. Toronto: Lester Publishing, 1994.

Koch, Tom. On the Subject(s) of Jack Kevorkian. *Cambridge Quarterly of Healthcare Ethics* 7, no. 4 (1998): 436–442.

Kübler-Ross, Elisabeth. (1988) *Living with Death and Dying*. New York: Macmillan

Laing, R. D. (1969) *Self and Others*. New York: Penguin Books.

Le Guin, Ursula K. (1929) The Space Crone. In *Dancing at the Edge of the World: Thoughts on Words, Women, Places*. New York: Grove/Atlantic, 1997.

Locke, Michelle. Tired Kin Opting to "Dump Granny." *Raleigh News & Observer*, November 28, 1991, B1.

Malinowski, M. J. Capitation, Advances in Medical Technology, and the Advent of a New Era in Medical Ethics. *American Journal of Law and Medicine* 22, nos. 2&3 (1996): 331–360.

McArthur, William J. Geriatric House Calls—Relic of the Past or Challenge of the Future? *Canadian Family Physician* (July 1991).

McCulloch, Robert G. Bone Measurement, Physical Activity, and the Aging Skeleton. *Canadian Journal of Aging* 15, no. 1 (1996): 54–64.

Minkler, Meredith, and Anne Robertson. The Ideology of "Age/Race" Wars: Deconstructing a Social Problem. *Aging and Society* 11, no. 1 (1991): 1–22.

Mitchell, Alanna. Seniors Gain at Expense of Young, Report Says. *Globe and Mail*, July 15, 1992, A7.

Muriel Spark. *Momento Mori*. New York: Macmillan, 1959.

Riabowol, Karl T. Editorial: Basic Biological Aging Research in Canada: Time for Rejuvenation? *Canadian Journal of Aging* 15, no. 1 (1996): 1–4.

Rile, Matilda W., Robert L. Kahn, and Anne Foner, Eds. (1994) *Age and Structural Lag: Society's Failure to Provide Meaningful Opportunities in Work, Family, and Leisure*. New York: John Wiley & Sons.

Rosenthal, M. L., ed. (1962) *Selected Poems and Two Plays of William Butler Yeats*. New York: Collier Books. 190–193.

Rowe, John W., and Robert L. Kahn. (1998) *Successful Aging*. New York: Pantheon. Also see, "How We Live Determines How We Age." *USA Today*, March 19, 1998, 80.

Sacks, Oliver. (1985) *The Man Who Mistook His Wife for a Hat*. New York: Summit Books.

Salholz, Eloise. Blaming the Voters; Hapless Budgeteers Single Out "Greedy Geezers." *Newsweek*, October 29, 116, no. 18 (1990): 36.

Somerville, Margaret A. Euthanasia by Confusion. *UNSW Law Journal* 20, no. 3 (1997): 1–20.

Terkel, Studs. (1967) *Division Street: America*. New York: Avon Books, prefatory notes.

Trotsky, Leon. (1935) *Trotsky's Diary in Exile*. Trans. Elena Zarudnaya. Cambridge, MA: Harvard University Press, 1976.

Woodward, Kathleen. (1991) *Aging and Its Discontents: Freud and Other Fictions*. Bloomington: Indiana University Press.

About the Author

TOM KOCH is a writer and researcher specializing in medical ethics and in public information theory. He is an adjunct professor of gerontology at Simon Fraser University and an associate of the Center on Aging, University of Hawaii. This is the third book in his trilogy on age and elder care; the earlier volumes are *Mirrored Lives: Aging Children and Elderly Parents* (Praeger, 1990) and *A Place in Time: Care Givers for Their Elderly* (Praeger, 1993).